ISBN 978-1-332-34115-3
PIBN 10316375

A SHORT MANUAL

OF

FOREST MANAGEMENT

CAMBRIDGE UNIVERSITY PRESS
C. F. CLAY, MANAGER
LONDON : FETTER LANE, E.C. 4

LONDON : WILLIAM WESLEY AND SON,
28 Essex Street, Strand, W.C. 2
NEW YORK : THE MACMILLAN CO.
BOMBAY }
CALCUTTA } MACMILLAN AND CO., LTD.
MADRAS }
TORONTO : THE MACMILLAN CO
OF CANADA, LTD.
TOKYO : MARUZEN-KABUSHIKI-KAISH

A SHORT MANUAL
OF
FOREST MANAGEMENT

BY

H. JACKSON, M.A.,
SCHOOL OF FORESTRY,
UNIVERSITY OF CAMBRIDGE

CAMBRIDGE
AT THE UNIVERSITY PRESS
1921

PREFACE

THE object of the present manual is to present a brief and simplified text-book on Forest Management, based on a purely practical foundation. The standard works on this subject sometimes present—for the student, and especially for the public—a rather formidable appearance, and contain an exposition of high theory a part of which at the present time is seldom, if ever, capable of practical application to the forest conditions of our own country, or of our possessions in other parts of the world. An attempt is made therefore to produce a simplified practical review of this subject from which are eliminated all reference to advanced theories which are not at present susceptible of practical application, and all other matters of purely academic interest. Some confusion has resulted, it is thought, in the past, from attempting to embrace in one study such diverse conditions as obtain in the most intensively worked continental forests which have been highly organised for generations, in the vast forests of India which are still generally in their natural state of the utmost irregularity, and thirdly in the small estate woodlands and plantations of our own country. An attempt is therefore made now to discriminate between such different types of forest with a view to elucidate and facilitate the preparation of suitable working-plans for each type.

Use has been made of the following standard works on Forest Management: *Manual of Forestry*, vol. III. Sir Wm. Schlich; *The Forester*, J. Nisbet; *The Practice of Forestry*, P. T. Maw; *British Estate Forestry*, A. C. Forbes; *Forest Working Plans in India*, W. E. D'Arcy.

H. JACKSON.

Jan. 1921

CONTENTS

CHAPTER V. GENERAL PRINCIPLES OF PLAN.

CHAPTER VI. METHODS OF TREATMENT.

CHAPTER VII. CALCULATION OF THE POSSIBILITY.

CHAPTER VIII. THE WORKING-PLAN REPORT.

CHAPTER IX. BRITISH ESTATE FORESTS.

DEFINITIONS

Block is a large natural subdivision of a forest, either formed by a detached group of woodland, or else a section of a main forest area determined by its situation, with natural boundaries, and often with a local name. It may be of any size and shape, and has nothing to do with the method of treatment.

Periodic block is a subdivision of a felling-series under the Uniform method: it contains a succession of age-classes generally extending over about twenty or thirty years, set apart to be regenerated during the corresponding period of the same duration. The whole felling-series or working-circle is divided into as many periodic blocks as the rotation is divided into periods.

Compartment is a permanent topographical subdivision of the block and forms the unit of area. Its boundaries are natural, or are formed by roads or lines.

Sub-compartment is an area in which the condition of the crop, its composition and age, and the soil and situation, are sufficiently homogeneous for each such unit of the crop to be capable of being described in one statement.

Coupe is an annual felling-area under the provision of the working-plan.

Normal forest is a forest which, in addition to being fully stocked, and yielding the maximum possible production of wood per acre per annum up to the limit imposed by the local conditions of soil and climate, is constituted of a complete and regular succession of age-classes, from one year old up to the age chosen as the rotation, with each age-class occupying an equal area.

In other words, the normal growing stock results from a normal succession of age-classes, with a normal increment. It is the ideal state of perfection in forest organisation; it is not absolute, but is relative to a given rotation and a given silvicultural method of treatment.

Constitution of a crop refers to the existence of a regular succession of age-classes in it.

Composition of a crop refers to the species that compose it.

Exploitability is the condition of a tree or crop that has reached the age or size at which it yields the kind of produce most useful to its owner, under the declared object of management.

Possibility is the maximum quantity of material, which may, for the time being, be annually removed from a forest, consistently with such treatment as shall tend to bring the forest as near as possible to the normal state, and with maintaining a constant yield.

Increment is the increase, due to growth, in the volume of material of a tree or crop, in a given time.

Working-circle is an area of the forest worked under one and the same method of treatment, with the same rotation, and the same set of prescriptions under one and the same working-plan.

Felling-series is an area of forest forming an entire working-circle, or else a section of a working-circle, containing a complete separate series of age-classes, thereby forming a miniature forest, and a unit of management complete in itself.

Cutting-series is a subdivision of a felling-series comprising a number of age-gradations differing in age by a constant number of years. The object is to break up the succession of coupes in order to reduce the danger of injury from wind. Instead therefore of a single succession of crops on the ground from one year old up to a hundred, the first cutting-series would contain—if there were five of them—crops aged 1, 6, 11, and so on up to 96, the second cutting-series 2, 7, 12... up to 97, and so on.

Felling-cycle is the time elapsing between two successive principal fellings in the same area, worked by the Selection method.

Rotation is the time elapsing between the creation of a crop and its removal; or in other words, the age at which the crop attains exploitability under the stated object of management.

Thinning is a cultural operation which consists in removing from out of a growing tree crop the stems becoming superfluous, so that, while realising these latter, each tree left standing may have sufficient space to attain that state of development which is required for it to satisfy the objects of management.

1. The basis of management.

Woods and forests, whether owned by private landlords, or by the State or other corporate bodies, must obviously be managed in such a way as to carry out as far as possible the wishes of the owner. The foundation of forest management therefore is the object of management as stated, after due consideration, by the owner of the forest. No one but the owner can decide authoritatively on the policy to be followed, and it is his duty and privilege therefore to think the matter out carefully, and then to define exactly what his object or objects is or are. Until this is done the professional forester can do little or nothing to help matters. In some cases, as in most State forests, the object of management has been definitely and explicitly laid down; but in others, notably in British estate woods, the object has never been clearly thought out nor defined, and is often, there is reason to fear, non-existent.

2. Various objects of management.

Speaking generally, these objects of management may be classified as being either physical or economic. The former class would apply generally to all forests of protection, such as forests maintained on mountain slopes to prevent erosion, ravinement, landslips or torrents, and to forests in the catchment areas of rivers affording an important water supply; and to any forests maintained for climatic reasons or other indirect effects. It would also apply to private woodlands attached to estates in Great Britain which are treated as amenity grounds for landscape or arboricultural purposes, and lastly also—at any rate to some extent—to woodlands worked primarily as game preserves. On the other hand, an economic object of management would apply to all forests of supply—to all forests, that is, which are worked mainly with a view to a supply of timber or other forest produce, which therefore form a commercial enterprise and occupy rent-yielding ground. In this case the owner would wish to adopt a scheme of management such as would primarily render his woodlands a financial success, yielding the maximum soil rental and giving him the highest net return on his invested capital.

In many cases it is of course possible to adopt a mixed object—at any rate to some extent—and so to modify the strict financial course in any given direction. Even game preserving is not altogether incompatible with economic forestry, though the fact that rabbits generally accompany pheasants makes it difficult. So, too, in the case of State forests, it may be the duty of the State to produce timber of the largest possible dimensions for the benefit of the community at large, since private owners cannot afford to work with such a long rotation, involving an immense invested capital and a proportionately diminished rate of interest. In this case the State would have to modify the strictly financial rotation, and deliberately to extend it in order to obtain the timber of large dimensions required by the general public.

3. Choice of species.

The object of management having been carefully considered, and definitely stated in precise terms, it is possible then to consider how this object may be best attained with reference to choice of species, choice of method of treatment, and choice of size of maturity. With regard to choice of species, if we are dealing with a large State forest of natural origin covering an extensive area, there may be no question as to species, nor possibility of making any direct alteration in this respect; but if on the other hand we are dealing with small woodland areas such as exist all over Great Britain, it may be quite possible to make a change from coniferous to broad-leaved species, or *vice versâ*, or to substitute one species for another, if by doing so, the objects of management, financial or economic, can be better realised. It is of course always safer to retain a species which is found growing naturally and healthily in its own habitat than to introduce a new—or still more an exotic—species, of which the future is necessarily uncertain and speculative. In any case the species chosen must always be absolutely suited to the local conditions of soil and climate in every respect. The advantages and disadvantages of pure and mixed crops may be considered at the same time, in relation to the silvicultural character and light requirements of the species in question. In most cases the nature of the soil and climate will indicate very plainly what species is best suited to it, and no other tree should then usually be considered.

4. Choice of silvicultural method.

Then as to silvicultural method. This will be controlled largely by the species with which we are dealing, and also by the length of rotation required to carry out the object of management; the timber market too will have to be consulted, and the requirements of local industries taken into account. These considerations will generally be sufficient to decide whether the system of high-forest should be adopted or not. If it is, the silvicultural character of the principal species and its light requirements will indicate whether the even-aged condition or that of mixed ages will be the more profitable. If natural regeneration by seed is practicable, this will be one of the most important points to be considered. In any case the choice of method must be based purely on silvicultural grounds, and no considerations, economic or financial, except in so far as they are in perfect harmony with the cultural requirements of the species, and the maintenance and improvement of the fertility of the soil, must be entertained for a moment.

5. Choice of rotation.

Then, lastly, as to the length of rotation. From the definition of the object of management it should be possible to deduce what size of timber it is necessary to turn out in order to attain that object. The timber market must be consulted, and the probable future demand estimated. On the other hand all available data as to the rate of growth of the species in question must be studied, and its periodic increment in volume, quality, and price, up to the age of its physical maturity. Such considerations will serve to determine—at any rate to within a period of a few years more or less—the age at which the desired size of tree may, under local conditions of soil and climate, be realised.

A longer rotation generally means a more valuable yield, but, on the other hand, it also means a larger wood-capital, and therefore a proportionately smaller rate of interest on the capital involved.

For forests of protection therefore, as we have already seen, as distinguished from forests of supply, a physical rotation would be adopted, while for ordinary commercial forests, the rotation corresponding to the maximum soil-rental expresses the true economic value of the management, but this is an exceedingly difficult matter to determine exactly. In the case of State forests, where the object of management is the production of timber of the largest possible dimensions, the rotation may be longer than the true financial rotation, while in the case of private forests worked for the production of small wood or fuel, the rotation adopted may be in the neighbourhood of the short rotation corresponding to the greatest production of volume, at the age when the current and mean annual rates of increment coincide. In any case cultural considerations have to be taken into account as well as economic ones.

6. Time element in forestry. The wood-capital.

THE preliminary matters discussed in the foregoing chapter having been settled, it now becomes necessary to consider the manner in which a forest may best be made to operate as a wood-producing and rent-yielding property, and to organise the working in such a way as to make the enterprise as profitable as possible.

The distinguishing characteristic of forestry is the time element. Instead of harvesting the fruit as it becomes ripe year by year, as is the case in agriculture, in forestry we may have to keep our trees standing for 100, or even 200, years, before they become mature. Then to ensure a proper condition of the ground, to make it suitable for reproduction by seed, and to secure the highest degree of productivity, it is necessary to maintain a more or less close leaf-canopy over it for the space of one to two human generations at least. It may be assumed that a yearly return is required, unless the woodland estate is too small to make an annual out-turn practicable. It may also be assumed that this annual return should be constant, that is, sustained at approximately the same figure year by year.

If then we have, for example, an area of 100 acres of woodland, worked on a 100-year rotation, we should be able to fell each year one acre of forest of one hundred years of age, which would give us our equal annual yield. But in order to do this in perpetuity, it would obviously be necessary to maintain standing the whole 100 acres stocked with a regular succession of crops, each crop occupying exactly the same area of one acre, and composed of ages forming an arithmetical series of 1, 2, 3, 4 years, and so on, up to 98, 99 and 100.

It is a requisite condition for the realisation of an equal annual yield that there should be this complete succession of equal areas of all age-classes, from one year old up to the age taken as the age of maturity—one area for each year of age—always kept standing, and fully stocked, up to the standard imposed by the local conditions of soil and climate.

Just before the 100-year-old acre of forest in the above example is felled, this acre may be regarded as the interest on the capital formed by the 99 acres of growing stock. Just as money deposited in a bank produces annual interest, so does our wood-capital standing in the forest. Instead, however, of harvesting each year the annual production of each acre of the forest, we realise each year the accumulated production (*e.g.*) of 100 years on one-hundredth part of the whole area; and we can only continue to do so permanently, if we maintain a complete and unbroken succession of all age-classes, each occupying an equal area, always standing and in active growth. See the figure on page 9.

It is evident that the longer the rotation, the greater will be the wood-capital or growing stock which it will be necessary to maintain. If, for instance, in the above example we were to make 200 years our rotation instead of 100, it is obvious that the volume of our wood-capital would have to be doubled, although the annual yield (200 years accumulated production over half an acre) would be much the same as before.

In systematic forestry therefore, where a sustained annual yield is desired, it is necessary to keep a very large volume of timber, covering a large extent of land, and representing a large amount of invested money, always standing on the ground. This graduated series of age-classes over equal areas is of course an artificial condition, and it may take as many years to constitute this wood-capital as there are years in the chosen rotation. The importance of the time element in forestry is thus easily felt, and the necessity for continuity of management is at once seen.

Without this continuity of management no organised forestry is possible, and that is one reason why working-plans have been generally confined to forests belonging to the State or other corporate bodies, in which some continuity is assured.

With private owners there is no assurance of continuity from one generation to another, and therefore the necessary organised growing stock is seldom, if ever, constituted, and systematic working is hardly possible.

Another point to be noted is that there is nothing but voluntary economic considerations by which to distinguish the wood-interest from the wood-capital, because they are identical in nature and are joined together. In the wood of any tree, the year's accretion of new wood, and the older wood which produced this accretion, are exactly alike and form one piece of wood. So, in the forest, there is nothing to distinguish how much is capital and how much is interest, except self-imposed moral considerations.

Consequently mistakes may be made which may take a lifetime to correct, and the wood-capital may be drawn upon for many years without any appreciable loss being felt, but at least as many years will have to be spent in re-accumulating the capital stock which has been wrongfully dissipated.

From these considerations, it is seen that the time element, and the largeness of the capital required to produce timber, and the danger of unbalancing the systematic management by liquidating a part of the capital, combine to render forestry more suitable to corporate bodies, which have an interest in continuity, than to private owners of limited means.

7. The normal forest.

In forest management the ideal condition is known as the "normal" forest, and a forest is said to be "normal," when, in addition to being constituted of a complete series of growths of all ages from the seedling to the exploitable tree, each age-class occupying an equal area, it is completely stocked, and the growth is proportionate to the fertility of the soil.

In other words, it is a forest formed of a regular succession of equal areas of each age-class, from one year old up to the age of the rotation adopted; it is fully stocked, and has no blanks, no defects or deficiencies, and the production of wood annually over every square foot of the area is the maximum quantity possible under the local conditions of soil and climate. It is the ideal state of perfection which is very seldom—if ever—realised in practice. It will be noticed that this normal state represents nothing absolute, but is merely relative to a given method of treatment and a given rotation. A forest might be normal under one rotation and one method of treatment, but it would at once become abnormal if either of these conditions was changed, and the forest required to be re-constituted or organised on a different pattern. Normal volume means the total cubic contents of the whole growing stock of a normal forest, which results from its being formed of a normal (that is, complete and regular, with an equal area of each) succession of age-classes, and from its having a normal increment, that is, a maximum possible annual rate of production. It is of course not necessary that the different age-classes should be arranged contiguously in regular succession of age on the ground, nor is it even necessary that each age-class should be contained on a single area all of one holding, but the normal state may, and always ought to, exist, even in an irregular forest, where trees of all ages are mixed up anyhow, and growing one above another all over the whole area, although in this case no separate age-classes are visible. Unless this normal series of age-classes exists—although invisible—the full equal yield cannot be realised every year for ever.

8. Relation between wood-capital and increment.

To make this clear, let us take an example. Suppose that we are working a forest on a twenty year rotation, and for that purpose have divided the ground up into twenty equal areas.

We can represent our growing stock diagrammatically as in the figure on page 9. The horizontal co-ordinate represents the area divided into 20 equal parts, and the vertical co-ordinate represents the volume of timber produced by the growth of the forest year by year. We have then 20 crops of equal area forming a regular succession of ages. The first area, on the left-hand side, is 1 year old, the second 2 years old, the third 3 years old, and so on up to the twentieth area which is 20 years old. The volume of the growing stock or wood-capital is represented by the area of the triangle *ABC*, and the yield, which is equal to the annual increment over the whole area, is represented by the rectangle *AEFB*, which is formed of 20 years' accumulated growth on one-twentieth of the area, and is equal to the sum of the annual increments (the portions shaded along the diagonal *AC*) for one year over the whole twenty sub-divisions of the area. We can now see the relation which necessarily exists between the increment and the growing stock. If the whole area were stocked with growth of 20 years of age, the volume of the wood-capital would be represented by the rectangle *ABCD*, so that our present normal wood-capital, represented graphically by the triangle *ABC*, is equal to one half the increment during the whole rotation over the whole area, or, in other words, it is equal to the average annual increment over the whole area during half the number of years in the rotation.

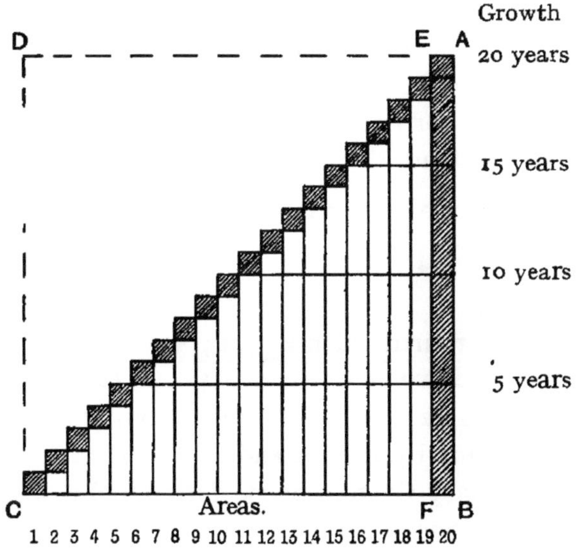

This essential relation may also be demonstrated in another way. In our example the growing stock is composed of the sum of an arithmetical series of crops of equal area aged 1, 2, 3, etc. years up to 20 years old. Then if the average annual increment, or production of cubic feet of wood, over the whole area, be indicated by I, and the rotation be indicated by r the wood-capital is equal to $\frac{I}{r} \times (1+2+3+\ldots+r)$

$$= \frac{I}{r} \times \frac{r.(r+1)}{2} = I \times \frac{r}{2} \text{ approximately.}$$

The normal growing stock is therefore equal to half the accretion taking place throughout the rotation over the whole area, the other half furnishing the yield during this time.

9. The quarter-girth convention.

THE cubic contents of a log of wood are found by multiplying the sectional area at the middle of the log, which presumablv tapers, more or less evenly, from one end to the other, by its length. In terms of the girth at the point where the sectional area is taken, this area equals $\frac{g^2}{4 \cdot \pi}$.

The volume in cubic feet therefore, if the girth is measured in inches and the length in feet, will be

$$\frac{g^2}{4 \cdot \pi} \times \frac{1}{144} \times \text{length}.$$

This will give the true volume.

For commercial purposes, however, the true contents are not calculated, but instead, the quarter-girth measure is employed.

In this method the sectional area is taken $\left(\frac{g}{4}\right)^2$, or, in other words, π is taken as 4.

Therefore,

$$\frac{\text{the quarter-girth volume}}{\text{the true volume}} = \frac{3 \cdot 14159}{4} = \frac{78 \cdot 5}{100} = \frac{113}{144},$$

and the true volume can be obtained from the quarter-girth measure by dividing by 113 instead of by 144.

Thus the ordinary Custom-house formula, by which import duty is levied on foreign timber, is

$$\frac{\left(\frac{g}{4}\right)^2 \times \text{length}}{113} = \text{true cubic feet}.$$

whereas the ordinary commercial Hoppus measure, which is $78\frac{1}{2}$ per cent. of the real contents, is

$$\frac{\left(\frac{g}{4}\right)^2 \times \text{length}}{144}.$$

In each case *g* is measured in inches at the middle of the log, and the length of the log, or the timber-height of the tree, is measured in feet.

As regards felled timber there is no difficulty about making the measurement. For the girth, a quarter-girth tape, or a string is used, while for the length an ordinary tape is used, or else a rod with feet marked on it. If the shape of the tree or log is in any way irregular, it is measured off into different sections of regular form, and each section is measured separately.

10. Commercial method of estimating standing timber.

With standing timber, there are two procedures to be considered; first the ordinary commercial method of calculation, and secondly the method employed for purposes of forest management, or for scientific investigations, in which the true volume is required.

By the commercial method, the girth is taken at 4 or 5 feet from the ground with a quarter-girth tape, which gives at once the quarter-girth to the nearest quarter of an inch.

The next step is to make a deduction for bark, which in most parts of the country is done by allowing one inch for every foot of quarter-girth. Thus if a tree measures anything under 24 inches of quarter-girth, but 18 inches or over, 1½ inches would be deducted for bark. An oak of course has a thicker bark than a beech, and an opportunity may offer of measuring what the actual thickness of bark is in a tree of any given species and any given size. The correct mathematical allowance is ·39 of an inch from the quarter-girth for every quarter of an inch of thickness of bark. Ordinarily, however, the commercial rule of thumb of ½ inch for every 6 inches of quarter-girth is followed.

The next step is to estimate the timber-height of the tree, that is, the length of bole from the base of the trunk up to the point at which the stem divides up into the main branches that form the lower part of the crown. This estimate is made by eye, without using any means of measuring the height. It requires practice and experience to do it accurately, and it is desirable always to stand at about the same distance from the tree when judging the height fit to yield sawing timber. There is of course no objection to making use of a long measured pole which can be held up against the trunk, to assist in estimating its height. It only remains now to make a further deduction from the quarter-girth under bark to allow for the taper of the stem. What is wanted is the quarter-girth under bark at mid-timber-height. Thus, suppose the timber-height is estimated at 50 feet, and we have taken the quarter-girth at 5 feet from the ground; we now have to estimate the deduction for taper to be made over a length of 20 feet, which is the distance through which we have to raise our point of girthing to arrive at the middle of the timber-length. The deduction to correspond with 20 feet of height would generally be about 3 inches, or something between 2 and 4 inches. Here again there may be an opportunity of measuring some felled trees lying on the ground to ascertain what degree of taper actually exists. It may vary very considerably according to the local conditions of growth, and especially with the density of the crop, and an error in estimating this deduction will make a considerable difference to the cubic contents.

Another point that requires to be fixed is—up to what size is to be considered measurable timber? Anything above 6 inches in diameter is usually considered as possible timber, or in the case of coniferous trees in regions where pitwood is saleable, the limit may be put at 3 inches diameter.

The quarter-girth under bark at mid-timber-height, and the timber-height, being now arrived at by this process of estimation, it is only necessary to turn up Hoppus's tables to ascertain the corresponding volume in cubic feet.

11. True measure of standing timber.

For purposes of forest management, and for scientific investigations, some more accurate means of ascertaining the true cubic contents of standing timber than the foregoing method, which relies too much on ocular estimates, must be employed.

In continental countries, where systematic forestry has been practised for a long time, and where careful data and statistics of all kinds have been recorded and accumulated for a long time, form-factors and volume-tables have been arrived at, which are most useful for these purposes, and are available now for each different species in each sort of locality, grown in each kind of crop, age, and so on, and are based on the records of thousands of measurements. In these tables, form-factors are given separately for each species, with different factors corresponding to differences in height.

Where such form-factors exist, and are reliable, it is only necessary to know the diameter at breast-height (4 feet 3 inches exactly), and the timber-height, measured by a dendrometer, thus:

Contents in cubic feet

$$= F.f \times \frac{(\text{Diam. at B.H. in ins.})^2}{144} \times \frac{\pi}{4} \times \text{height},$$

which would be equivalent to

$$\frac{(\text{Diam. in ins. at mid-timber-height})^2}{144} \times \frac{\pi}{4} \times \text{height},$$

or

$$\frac{(\text{Girth at mid-timber-height in ins.})^2}{144} \times \frac{1}{4 \cdot \pi} \times \text{timber height in feet.}$$

It is of course only in very uniform crops grown in fully stocked, close-canopied high-forest that form-factors and volume-tables, which generally refer to the height of the tree, could be safely applied, and even then they would only give good results when applied to a large number of trees.

However, for the present we must generally be content to do without these convenient helps to investigations regarding the volume of standing timber, and find some other means of estimating the cubic contents of a standing crop. This is best done by finding out the exact size of a sufficient number of sample trees; and then to fell several trees of these sizes, and cut them into small sections, and measure them carefully, timber and branch-wood.

The usual procedure is as follows. An enumeration is made of the trees forming the crop, which are then totalled up for each size class—generally 1-inch diameter-classes, or 3-inch girth-classes—and the size-classes are grouped together so as to form say from three to six groups of equal range: the basal area corresponding to each size is taken from tables, and entered in a column against that class, so that by multiplying this basal area by the number of trees in each size-class, and adding them together, the aggregate basal area of each group is found. Dividing this total by the number of trees in the group, the basal area of the average tree of the group is found, and its corresponding girth or diameter is taken from the tables. This gives us the exact size of the sample trees which we now have to find in the crop, and one or two sample trees as nearly as possible of exactly this size are selected for each group, and felled and cut up and carefully measured. This gives the cubic contents in timber and in small wood of the average tree for each group. This volume, multiplied by the proportion borne by the basal area of the whole group to the basal area of the sample trees felled and measured, gives the volume for each group in solid cubic feet. These have only to be totalled to get the total volume for the whole area enumerated. Columns can, if desired, be added for height, age, and form-factor.

This procedure would not be practicable in a very mixed and utterly irregular crop, as it assumes a certain degree of uniformity. If the crop were quite irregular in all respects, no accurate estimate could be arrived at except by estimating the volume of each tree separately.

If, on the other hand, the crop were practically even-aged and quite uniform, it would not be necessary to make groups, but one average tree for the whole crop could be taken. It will be noticed in the method described that no account is taken of height. If, however, the crop contains distinct height-classes, these must be dealt with separately in the same way.

Lastly, it is to be noted that, apart from the question of girth or diameter, care must be taken in selecting the sample tree, as any tree of this size would not do. It must be a tree representing in shape and development all the conditions of growth existing in the crop, especially with respect to the result of the density of the crop and the crowding together of the stems in their growth. The average density of the crop is of course a matter of first importance as determining the size, shape, and development, of the representative sample tree.

If the woodland area dealt with is of small extent, a complete enumeration would be made over the whole area. If, on the other hand, the forest is too large for a complete enumeration to be practicable, the estimate of its volume may be made either by linear surveys or by sample plots. In either case at least 5 per cent. of the area should be enumerated in order to obtain reliable results; less in young and regular crops, and more in old and irregular ones. Linear surveys are preferable to sample plots if the crop is irregular, or the ground hilly. In such a case a gridiron of lines of one or two chains in width should be taken right across the map in parallel lines at right angles to the contour lines as far as possible, or in both directions at right angles to one another. If sample plots are chosen, small areas of not less than half an acre in extent should be selected at various points in the forest so as to give a correct representation of all varieties of soil, situation, age, and condition of crops over the whole area.

12. Weise's method of finding the average tree.

Another method of finding the average tree in a fairly regular crop with a close canopy is Weise's. An enumeration of all stems on the area is made by 1-inch diameter or 3-inch girth-classes, and the number of stems is then totalled. A count-back of 40 per cent. of this total number of the trees is made beginning from the largest size. The size-class into which this count-back leads will contain the average stem of the whole crop. A few sample trees of this size should then be selected, felled, cut up, and measured.

13. Increment.

In order to ascertain what financial return is being obtained from the capital invested in a forest, and in order to frame a plan on business principles, it is necessary to know the increment in volume, quality, and price that is taking place at any given time.

For this purpose we have to find out the volume increment per acre per annum that is accruing in a standing crop of trees.

There is the rare case in which we might happen to have accurate measurements of the crop previously taken, with which, after a known period of years, we could easily ascertain the past rate of growth by comparing its present volume with its recorded volume in the past, but it is of course most unlikely that such past measurements will often be available. It will therefore be necessary generally to estimate the volume increment of the standing crop by means of the ascertained volume increment of an average sample tree, which, growing in a fully-stocked close-canopied crop, may be taken as representative of the entire crop.

It is obvious that our sample tree must represent all the general conditions of growth which govern the individual stems forming the crop, with a given degree of density, and growing in close cover, because a tree growing in a free and isolated position with an unrestricted amount of growing space in which to spread itself, will develop in a very different way from a stem grown in close cover. Then we have to remember that the determination of the past rate of increment, although—unlike the estimation of future increment, which is necessarily more or less speculative,—it rests on actual existing data, is complicated by the fact that a certain number of stems disappear out of the crop year by year, or are removed by thinnings, and that the stems remaining give us practically no information on this point.

The first thing to be done in any case is to consider the best means of ascertaining the rate of volume increment of a sample tree, which depends on its rate of growth in height, its form factor, and its rate of growth in basal area, which in turn is proportional to the square of its girth, diameter or radius. This volume increment may be expressed either in cubic feet, or else as a percentage. With reference to the volume of the wood-capital producing it, the increment of a whole crop is stated as so much per acre per annum.

14. Increment of felled trees. Stem-analysis.

In the case of felled trees, or of a sample tree which can be felled and cut up in order to measure its past-rate of growth in height and in radius, the rate of growth is ascertained by counting and measuring the annual rings.

The most complete investigation of this kind is effected by making what is called a stem-analysis, which is a rather intricate method of representing graphically the whole life-history of the tree's growth in height, radius, and volume. It is only used for purposes of scientific investigation.

In order to make a stem-analysis, the tree is cut up into a number of sections of, say, 10 feet in length; each section is then sawn across the middle, and the number of concentric rings exposed at each cross-section is successively counted and recorded.

From this record a table is prepared showing the number of years that it took the tree to grow to the height of 5, 15, 25, etc., feet, up to its present total height. These results are plotted in such a way as to represent graphically a longitudinal section of the tree. A vertical line represents the axis of the tree, with the heights of the successive cross-sections marked on it, and also the heights which the tree had reached at successive periods of its life.

Then at each cross-section the total number of annual rings is counted, and each ten years' growth in radius, working backwards towards the centre of the tree, is accurately measured in inches to two places of decimals, and a table is made of these measurements at each cross-section. These radii corresponding to successive ages are then plotted on a series of horizontal axes corresponding to the successive heights of the various cross-sections up to the top of the tree, and the points thus obtained are connected by lines which represent the stem curves during the life of the tree. A calculation can now be made of the volume of the tree at each decennial period, and a series of tables is prepared, giving the volume of each section at each age.

The periodic increment in cubic feet for every ten years is thus known, and a curve can be plotted, with cubic feet represented by the vertical axis, and age by the horizontal axis, showing the volume all through the life-time of the tree.

15. Increment of standing trees.

In the case in which the cubic contents of a certain tree-crop had been accurately measured n years ago, and were found to be v, while the present volume of the same crop is now V, the average annual increment will be $\frac{V-v}{n}$, and the mean volume of

the crop in the middle of the period of n years will be $\frac{V+v}{2}$.
If p is the percentage rate of increment, $p : 100 :: \frac{V-v}{n} : \frac{V+v}{2}$

therefore $p = 100 \times \frac{V-v}{n} \times \frac{2}{V+v} = \frac{200}{n} \times \frac{V-v}{V+v}$. Now if—as in practice is most probable—the crop we are investigating is a middle-aged one, and if the two periods are not separated by a great number of years, say more than ten years, in that case the height and the form-factor of the average sample tree will remain unchanged throughout the entire period of measurement, and the volumes will then be proportionate to the basal areas of the average sample tree of the crop, and the formula will take the form of

$$p = \frac{200}{n} \times \frac{D^2 - d^2}{D^2 + d^2}.$$

As the difference between the two diameters will be small, $D^2 + d^2$ will be approximately the same as $\frac{1}{2}(D + d)^2$, and so the formula can be simplified to the form

$$p = \frac{200}{n} \times \frac{D-d}{D+d}.$$

16. Pressler's formula.

This formula of Pressler's is a very useful one, and may be relied upon to give good results, provided that the crop be of middle age, say, of at least sixty years old, and that n represents a small number of years so that D and d do not differ greatly.

In the case of standing timber, the radial increment of the tree is readily ascertained by means of Pressler's borer. This is a tool like a hollow gimlet, which is screwed into the sample tree in a radial direction at right angles to the axis of the tree, and which thereby extracts a round spill of wood about 2 inches in length from the tree. To insure accuracy two, if not four, borings at right angles to one another should be made at the same level on each tree; the annual rings on the spills of wood extracted will be carefully counted and measured, and the mean taken.

17. Schneider's formula.

Another very useful formula is Schneider's. Suppose that D is the mean diameter of the sample tree at breast-height, and that n is the number of annual rings in the last inch of radius, and let us suppose also that the diameter D lies, not outside, but in the middle of the 1-inch zone of increment resulting from the n years' growth. The area of this zone of increment is

$$\frac{\pi}{4}.(D+1)^2 - \frac{\pi}{4}.(D-1)^2 = \frac{\pi}{4}.4D = \pi.D,$$

and the annual increment of this basal area will be $\frac{\pi.D}{n}$: then, assuming that the increment takes place half inside and half outside the present diameter,

$$p : 100 :: \frac{\pi.D}{n} : \frac{\pi.D^2}{4}$$

and $$p = \frac{400}{n.D}.$$

Schneider's formula gives practically the same result as Pressler's, for if in the latter n be taken as 1 year, the $D - d$ = twice the breadth of the last ring, and $D + d$ = twice the present diameter, so

$$p = 400 \times \frac{\text{breadth of the last ring}}{\text{breadth of the present diameter}},$$

which is the same result as is given by Schneider's formula.

18. Breymann's formula.

A third formula of the same kind which is often useful for purposes of investigation of increment is Breymann's. In this, the width of the last annual increase of the diameter d is represented by a, so that $\frac{a}{2}$ represents the last annual increase of radius, and here again we will suppose that the diameter d lies in the middle of this zone of increment. The superficial area of the last annual zone of increment is

$$\frac{\pi}{4} \times \left\{\left(d+\frac{a}{2}\right)^2 - \left(d-\frac{a}{2}\right)^2\right\} = \frac{\pi}{4}.2.a.d = \pi.d \times \frac{a}{2}$$

then $$p : 100 :: \pi.d.\frac{a}{2}\ \frac{\pi.d^2}{4}$$

and $$p = 200 \times \frac{a}{d}.$$

This formula gives the current annual percentage increment of basal area at breast-height (and also in cubic contents of the tree) as equal to $200 \times \frac{a}{d}$, while the diametral increment of any stem is found in the proportion of

$$p : 100 :: a : d, \text{ or } p = 100 \times \frac{a}{d}.$$

Comparing these two results it becomes evident that the percentage increment in basal area of the stem, and in the cubic contents of the tree, is always twice as great as the percentage of increment in diameter.

Schneider and Breymann's formula only give the current annual percentage of increase during the year of investigation, while Pressler's gives it for a short period of, say, ten years, either past, present, or future.

All three formulae rest on breast-height diameter of standing timber, and assume that height and form-factor remain the same for both periods. Therefore, to ensure accuracy, it is better, when practicable, to fell a few average sample trees, and then to cross-cut them at mid-height, measure the annual rings at the mid-section, and then calculate the current percentage increment by Schneider's formula. In cases of appreciable height growth, the formulae for breast-high diameter should be enhanced by a small percentage of up to 25 per cent.

19. Increment of whole crops.

We have already seen that the past increment of a wood cannot accurately be deduced from the results of an investigation into the rate of growth of single trees, as many stems will have disappeared or been removed in the thinnings. The past increment of middle-aged and older woods will therefore be less than that of the single average tree.

This difficulty, however, does not present itself so much in the case of the present and future increments, especially when we only estimate such increment for a short term of years for practical purposes of management, and in such cases it is safe to assume that for the next ten years the increment of the crop will be about the same as during the last similar period.

For a whole wood, the present annual increment may be roughly obtained by the formula $p = 100 \times \frac{\text{mean annual increment}}{\text{present cubic contents}}$ when the mean annual increment is found by dividing the present volume of the growing stock by its age, and this method would give fair results in the case of a middle-aged crop that has just passed its maximum mean annual increment. If the volume of the crop has been calculated by forming groups of diameter-classes, the mean percentage of increment should be estimated for each group from sample trees of that group, and then the current annual increment in cubic feet will be estimated for each size-class, and the sum of them added together will give the increment of the whole crop.

A comparison of the course of the current annual increment per acre with the mean annual increment $\left(= \frac{\text{volume}}{\text{age}}\right)$ during the life-time of a crop will always yield information useful for purposes of forest management. Curves to indicate the current and mean increments may be plotted, with a horizontal co-ordinate for age, and a vertical co-ordinate to represent cubic feet of increment year by year. These increment curves must not be confused with volume curves. The current increment rises rapidly at first, and reaches its maximum towards the end of the pole stage, when the height-growth culminates; earlier on good soils, and with light-demanding species. It then falls gradually. The mean annual increment rises more slowly, and reaches its maximum often about thirty or forty years later, and it is at its maximum when it is equal to the current annual increment. It is at this period that the production of volume per acre per annum is at its maximum. Later on the mean increment gradually decreases, but much less rapidly than the current increment.

A single tree growing in a free open position would have a higher increment than an average tree grown in a close crop, but the fully-stocked wood would have a larger increment per acre than the open wood, because the number of stems is so much greater, although the crowding diminishes the growth in diameter.

20. Yield-tables.

Lastly, for fully-stocked crops that may be considered as fairly normal, the increment past, present and future, may be obtained from average yield-tables, in countries where such yield-tables exist.

Yield-tables are constructed by measuring a very large number of woods of all different ages, normal sample plots fully stocked, of all species and qualities, and then plotting the volumes thus obtained by means of co-ordinates indicating cubic feet vertically and age horizontally. The outside points, that is, the highest and lowest volumes recorded, are connected severally by two curves, and the intermediate space is divided into three or four equal strips through the middle of which a line is drawn to represent the mean volume curve for each of the three or four quality classes.

A tabular statement of this kind for each species shows the course of development of a wood throughout its life-time, under each quality of soil and climate, and under each method of treatment, and affords average statistics for each unit of area, at every age, as to the number of trees, their mean height, diameter, volume, increment and form-factor. Such yield-tables which afford information which is indispensable for a full and proper knowledge of all the economic and financial questions which have to be dealt with in forest management, may be either general or local.

21. Preliminary examination of the area.

THE object of the field work to be carried out in connection with the preparation of a working-plan is to examine the forest and make a classified inventory of the crops, and to investigate the local conditions of growth, in order to collect data on which to base prescriptions for the future organisation and management of the area. The results of these investigations will then be incorporated into a detailed statistical report which will form the first part of the working-plan report.

The first step will be to make a preliminary reconnaissance of the whole area, and then to proceed to the collection of statistical details with regard to the topography, the configuration of the ground, the soil, and climate, including a report on the existing boundaries, and on the present system of roads, rides, etc. A review will then be made of any local requirements or agricultural customs likely to influence the management of the forest, and of any existing rights of any kind with which the forest area is burdened.

With regard to the soil, the physical and chemical characters both of soil and subsoil will have to be described, with the average depth, porosity, humidity, and the existence and quantity of vegetable matter in the surface soil, and the nature of the vegetable covering. Then, with regard to climate, particulars are required in connection both with the general and the local climate. The relative elevation of parts of the ground over the surrounding areas will have to be stated as well as the absolute altitude above sea-level.

The aspects have to be noted, and the average annual rainfall, the general state of humidity of soil and atmosphere, the force and direction of the prevailing winds, the occurrence of frosts in and out of season, and any other climatic influences. From the above information, taken in conjunction with indications afforded by the growth of the crops, especially in the matter of height-growth, it will then be possible to determine a site quality for each component part of the area.

22. General description of crop.

It will now be possible to proceed to a general description of the forest crop. The distribution and area of the different types of growth, and their suitability to the local conditions of soil and climate. The composition of the crops, the principal species and their relative proportions: their size and rate of growth, reproduction, and general conditions of vegetation. Then the constitution of the forest crop, that is, the relative proportions of the various size or age-classes. Any deficiency or irregularity in the succession of these classes should be noted, and, if possible, explained. The origin and past history of the forest crop should be stated, as well as the general density of stocking. Blanks and areas out of production should be noted, and lastly the effects of climatic influences such as altitude, wind, drought, frost, and the danger of injuries from insects and other pests, fire, etc. should be described.

At this stage it may be possible to note at once some obvious improvements that might be made in the selection of species, or in the choice of silvicultural method, in order to carry out the declared objects of management under the local conditions of soil and climate that have just been investigated.

23. The block.

The next subject to which attention has to be paid is the division of the forest into subdivisions. These may be either purely topographical, and therefore more or less natural and permanent, or they may be artificial, and dependant on the organisation of the area with a view to its working under a definite plan. Some existing subdivisions of the area will have been already made use of for the purpose of describing the soil, climate and crops, as indicated in the foregoing paragraphs. The topographical and permanent subdivisions of a forest are the block and the compartment. The block is a large natural subdivision of a forest, formed either of a detached and self-contained group of woodland, or else of a section of the main forest area, in which case it may often consist of one drainage basin and be bounded by a watershed. In any case, the block has natural boundaries such as watersheds, rivers, or roads, and it is often distinguished by a local name. It may be of any size and shape, and has no connection with the system adopted for working the forest.

24. The compartment.

The compartment is a subdivision of the block and forms the permanent unit of area. In a British woodland a compartment may be 10 acres in extent, and in a forest in Burma it may be 1000 acres. It depends on the size of the forest and the intensity of working. Its shape should be compact and more or less rectangular. Its boundaries will be formed by natural features of the ground, or by roads, rides, fire-lines, rivers, ridges, or, if necessary, by artificial lines.

25. The sub-compartment.

So far we have considered the compartment merely as a unit of area, but we also have to find a unit of the crop which has to be analysed and split up into silvicultural units. These will therefore have to consist of subdivisions of the forest in which the condition of the crop, its composition and age, and the soil and situation, are sufficiently homogeneous for each of them to be described as one unit of the crop. Now if the compartments are small and are formed by the regular intersection of a network of roads and lines, it is quite possible that the compartments already formed in this way will also serve effectively as silvicultural units for the purpose of affording a descriptive inventory of the crop. It will, however, often be necessary to subdivide our topographical compartments, because there will be found notable variations in soil, or situation, or in the species, age or condition of the crop. These subdivisions will be called sub-compartments. They are not necessarily permanent, because they are based on the nature of the crop standing on them at the present time. The whole forest is thus split up into silvicultural units, of no fixed size, but each containing a timber-crop capable of being included in, and covered by, one description.

This description of compartments and sub-compartments often forms the bulkiest part of the whole working-plan report, in which it is usually given as an Appendix. Its bulk, however, will never exceed its importance, as it forms the foundation for the whole enterprise, and will be found very valuable for future reference.

26. Description of compartments.

This description of compartments will be drawn up in tabular form, but will be written in narrative form under each heading. The headings will be area, soil and situation, description of the growing stock, and a column for remarks. Under description of the growing stock, the composition, age, and condition of the crop, will be given and an analysis and estimate of its contents. The site quality, and the density may be also given. Under remarks, notes will be made of any outstanding feature of each crop, of any cultural operations that seem to be called for, and suggestions regarding future treatment. There will of course be considerable variations in the scope of these descriptions, according to the extent of the area, the intensity of management, the method of treatment, and the nature of the crop.

27. Collection of statistical data.

In order to collect all the information required for this detailed description of sub-compartments it will be necessary to go all over the ground very carefully, and to note all differences occurring from point to point in the local conditions influencing the growth of the crop, such as soil and aspect. It will be necessary now to make careful note especially of the height-growth as indicative of the quality of the soil, of the conditions controlling regeneration, and of the cultural requirements of the different species, of which the relative proportions will also be recorded. The predominant age of each crop, the existence of over-mature stock, and the relative proportions of each component age-class should also be noted, together with the density of stock in each part.

In producing a working-plan it is the duty of the writer to set forth and bring up to date all statistical data regarding the local conditions of growth. Probably there will be a certain amount of information already recorded, and there may be sample plots for the periodical measurement of girth-growth of numbered sample trees already established. During the present detailed examination of the growing stock there should be a valuable amount of statistical figures obtained, such as careful measurements of the cubic contents of sample trees, ring countings, borings with Pressler's borer, and calculations of current and mean annual increment. All these investigations should be worked out and the results tabulated, and incorporated as appendices in the plan under preparation.

28. Formation of working-circles.

We now have to consider the subdivision of the area in relation to its organisation for the purpose of systematic working under a definite plan. A working-plan may be prepared for an estate or district containing woodland areas of diverse kinds, as for instance coniferous woods worked as high-forest, and broad-leaved woods worked as coppice-with-standards, requiring altogether different treatment. The first step to be taken then is to divide the area up into working-circles, each of which will be composed of an area of forest worked under one and the same method of treatment, with the same rotation, and the same set of rules, under the provisions of one working-plan.

29. Formation of felling-series.

The boundaries of the different working-circles having been determined, it may be found that for working purposes the areas so defined are inconveniently large. Instead therefore of working the whole area under one set of fellings, it may be advantageous from several points of view to divide the working-circle up into felling-series, each of which will be a unit area of working. The advantages of this arrangement are, better protection against wind and insects, increased facilities for the distribution of the produce to different centres of consumption, distribution of work among establishments, and improved conditions with regard to supervision and transport. The subdivision of the working-circle into felling-series makes no difference to the plan; it merely means that, for example, instead of felling every year one compact area of 500 acres, we are going to fell every year five different areas of 100 acres, each located in a different part of the forest. Each felling-series will be a complete and self-contained miniature of the whole working-circle, and should contain therefore as nearly as possible an equal area of every age-class. The number of series determined on will fix the size of the annual felling area in each series, and this number will be chosen, after due consideration of the questions above indicated, namely protection against wind or insects, distribution of produce in different directions, export and supervision, so as to produce manageable coupes of the most convenient size.

CHAPTER V. GENERAL PRINCIPLES OF PLAN.

30. The three types of forest.

BEFORE proceeding to consider the measures necessary for the detailed organisation of a forest under any definite method of treatment, it may assist a clearer understanding of the matters under discussion, from a practical point of view, if we now make some discrimination between the different stages of forest organisation that we may have to deal with, and distinguish two or three types of forest for which a working-plan may have to be prepared.

First of all then we have the rare case of the second or later rotation of a completely constituted forest, which has already been under intensive management for a long time, and which is as nearly normal (in the strict sense of the word, which should never be used in any other sense) as possible in every respect, so that the sustained yield is equal to the full normal increment. Such a forest could only be found in continental Europe, where intensive management has been carried out for several generations, and where financial and actuarial methods have been applied in great detail. This type of forest is the only one in which the normal idea comes within the immediate range of practical politics, in which valuations based on the maximum expectation value of the soil are possible, and in which yield-tables, increment-tables, and form-factors, are fully available. It is safe to say that no such forest exists in Britain or in any British possession at the present time.

Secondly we have the more common type of a forest fairly well stocked, and containing some faint resemblance to a succession of age-classes, but incomplete, and not regularly constituted, having not yet gone through a complete rotation under the present scheme of management, or perhaps now undergoing conversion from irregular to even-aged high-forest. During the first rotation (or, in the case of a selection forest, the first few felling-cycles) the building up of a complete and properly constituted growing stock is the principal thing aimed at, and regular working and full production will not be possible till after the end of the first rotation at the earliest. Meanwhile the yield will be based—not on any abstract theories as to normal increment—but on an estimate of the volume of standing old stock that has to be cleared off the ground period by period.

Lastly we have the case of our English woodland estates, where in most instances there is no assured continuity of management, and no very definite or stable object of management. A working-plan here will hardly touch the theories of forest management, but will rather be a common-sense plan of operations, with a progressive annual programme for the clearing and re-stocking of successive portions of the ground as rapidly as possible, so arranged that the receipts from clearings may cover the annual expenditure in re-planting.

31. General and special plan.

Whatever method of silvicultural treatment is to be adopted, the main provisions of the working-plan will take the form of a general working scheme followed by a special plan.

The general scheme will apply to the whole rotation, which, in high-forest, may be 100 or 200 years, and will embrace in outline the whole cycle of operations extending over that time.

The special plan will refer to a period generally of between ten and thirty years, and all the detailed prescriptions of the plan will remain in force only for this period. In the case of even-aged high-forest, one period, that is usually about twenty or thirty years, will be taken as the duration of the prescriptions of the plan; and the same period would be taken in the case of a plan of conversion to even-age high-forest. In high-forest of mixed ages, the period chosen for the duration of the special plan would be one felling-cycle, or, if the felling-cycle were very short—of not more than ten years, for instance—two felling-cycles might be taken. In the case of coppice the general working scheme and the special plan would practically coincide, and the duration of the plan would be for one rotation of the coppice.

While the general working scheme gives the framework of the whole proposition, the special plan gives full details regarding everything that has to be carried out in the forest during this first period of twenty or thirty years, during which time all its prescriptions remain in force. This includes a felling table showing exactly what area is to be felled each year, and the order of the annual coupes, if they exist; the nature of the fellings, and a set of cultural rules to guide the operator who carries them out; and lastly the material to be removed. This special plan therefore contains the gist of the whole document.

32. Duration of plan.

Now to attempt to make any detailed forecast as to the future condition of a forest after the lapse of a century or two, that is to say any forecast that can be put into figures—either as regards cubic contents or money value—is futile and misleading: if we are wise, we shall avoid mathematics based on unknown future conditions, and be content with a hope that, when that remote time arrives, the forest will be to some extent improved as the result of the wisdom of our present intervention. All calculations of every kind should be limited to the period of twenty or thirty years which has been adopted as the duration of the prescriptions of the plan. No attempt should be made to extend any hard-and-fast regulations for a longer future period, nor should any regulation of the yield be imposed as a binding prescription for more than twenty, or, at the outside, thirty, years.

It will in fact be found to be a wise course to follow if it is always provided that the calculations on which the regulation of the yield is based be revised every ten years, and that the working-plan itself be revised at the end of each period of twenty or thirty years, as the case may be.

Thirty years seems a short part of the life of a high-forest timber crop, but it is a man's whole working lifetime, and some progress should be made, and some improvements found available for introduction in the plan at the end of this period of inception.

33. Degree of rigidity desirable.

There is one point of general application that may be noted here, and that is that a fair margin of detail should always be left to the discretion of the local forester who has to carry out the prescriptions of the plan, and who may be assumed to be a fairly competent person.

Cultural considerations should always be recognised as paramount, and must take priority over all rules. This is an important principle, which must never be overlooked. For example, the cultural requirements of a timber crop must never be sacrificed for any paper calculations to regulate the yield, and no tree should ever be felled—notwithstanding any working-plan rule—if it is desirable for cultural reasons (such as shelter, or the production of seed, etc.) to keep it standing.

The local forester is in the best position to appreciate these cultural necessities, and therefore the prescriptions of the working-plan should never be so detailed, and so rigid, as to allow the local operator no discretionary power at all. Therefore, while the general organisation of the forest and the annual plan of operations are clearly and definitely laid down in the plan, cultural details should be indicated in such a way that the forester in charge will be at liberty to use his own judgment in carrying them out.

The terms employed in framing the prescriptions of the plan should, however, be precise and imperative. Suggestions and recommendations are generally out of place in a plan, because what is required are binding orders. "At such a place, at such a time, such and such an operation *will be carried out.*" Then no evasion, or deviation from the plan, is possible without special permission from competent authority. The working of the forest should be rigidly prescribed in explicit and uncompromising terms, while at the same time a fair margin of detail should be left to the discretion of the local forester. For example, suppose that, in prescribing the number of standards per acre to be reserved in a coppice, it is found that forty-five would be the best number to keep, in such a case the rule would be worded as follows: "Between forty and fifty standards will be reserved per acre." The framer of the rules should remember to look at them from the point of view of the local operator who will have to carry them out: the rules should be reasonable and easy to apply, without being weak or ambiguous. Conditional or facultative prescriptions may be employed in special cases to meet doubtful contingencies, but such should be clearly stated. The conduct of all essentially cultural operations, as for example the successive regeneration fellings in even-aged high-forest, must always be left to the local forester.

CHAPTER VI. METHODS OF TREATMENT.

34. Classification of methods.

THE methods of treatment that we now have to consider may be roughly classified as follows:

Permanent	Coppice system	Simple coppice
		Coppice-with-standards
	High-forest system	Even-aged
		Mixed ages
Provisional		Conversions
		Improvement.

35. Simple coppice.

In simple coppice the working-plan is of the simplest description, and consists in dividing the area of the working-circle, or of a felling-series forming a subdivision of the working-circle, into as many equal or equiproductive areas as there are years in the coppice rotation. One annual area is then cut each year in rotation. The number of years chosen as rotation depends on the size of produce required, and on silvicultural considerations. A few simple rules for the fellings will generally be drawn up in order to prescribe the manner of cutting the underwood and the season of cutting it. The rotation being short, generally between ten and twenty years, there will be no need as a rule for tending operations, but if, for instance, a cleaning at mid-rotation is thought desirable, in order to protect any seedling plants that may appear on the ground or for any other purpose, a prescription to this effect will be inserted.

The yield being determined by area, there will be no need to estimate the possibility in volume. During the first rotation there will probably be some irregularities to be faced. Some coupes may have to be felled when they are a few years older or younger than the proper age, but the main thing is to establish a regular succession of graded ages year by year, with equal areas of each, for the second and subsequent rotations. To obtain equal areas of all ages it might, for example, be wise to fell an area in the first year and then again a second time in the last year of the first rotation. In any case the areas must be classified by age, and a felling-table then made out so as to deal with them in such a way that at the end of the first rotation there will be left standing on the ground a complete series of all ages occupying equal areas. The actual out-turn year by year during the first rotation is not of first importance, and equality of yield for these first few years must be sacrificed to obtain the future regular constitution of the series.

36. Coppice-with-standards.

In the case of coppice-with-standards, the general arrangement will be the same as with simple coppice, and the size of the annual coupe will be found by dividing the area of the working-circle, or felling-series, by the number of years in the rotation, which in this case will often be about ten years longer than in simple coppice.

This rotation will have to be carefully considered from the point of view of the objects of management, of the size and quality of the produce required, and of the cultural character of the species concerned, in given conditions of soil and climate, with reference to both underwood and standards, since these latter too will be materially affected by the length of the coppice rotation, of which their ages will be a multiple.

In addition, the working-plan must regulate the selection and reservation of the standards. Here we must go back to the object of management as regards the reservation of standards, before we can decide anything as to the number and kind of trees to be reserved. Generally speaking, the object will either be a cultural one, such as the protection of the underwood against frost, or else an economic one, such as the production of timber of fair size. These two cases must be considered separately. In either case we propose to grow two kinds of crop on the same ground, while the available amount of soil and sunshine is strictly limited. The more standards we keep standing, the less coppice production per unit of area will be obtainable; so that the two things have to be weighed, the one against the other.

Now if the main object of the reservation of the standards be to protect the underwood from exposure and to supply seed, and the underwood is to be looked upon as the more important of the two kinds of crop, then the number of standards should be fixed so as just to effect these cultural objects, and should be kept at a minimum. The number should be no greater than what would ordinarily be sufficient for these purposes. But if on the other hand the object of maintaining an overwood is to produce timber, then in this case the value and importance of the standards will far outweigh that of the underwood, and the interest of the owner will demand the largest number of standards possible, without impairing the vigour of the coppice, which will still be the main agent of the perpetuation of the forest. These principles will be sufficient to enable us to decide on the best number of standards to keep. The upper limit, that is, the maximum possible number of standards, is fixed by the fact that if the overwood forms close canopy, the underwood will languish and tend to disappear. The rule therefore is that the standards must never be so numerous that each tree is not in a state of complete isolation, even at the end of the rotation, just before the felling is made. As soon as the crowns of the standards begin to touch one another, the coppice is in danger.

It will not be necessary each time to make a calculation as to the superficial cover of each size of reserved tree. As a general rule the standards will stand over one quarter, or as a maximum, one third of the area, and local experience will generally be available to assist one in deciding on the right number of standards per acre. The light-requirements of the species concerned, and in particular the amount of shade thrown by the species forming the overwood will of course affect the question. Then there is the further matter of the number of rotations during which a certain proportion (and what proportion?) of the reserves are to be kept standing. It is not often that a standard can be profitably kept for more than four or five coppice rotations. Here again the size and age of the kind of timber required under the object of management must be referred to, and at the same time it must be remembered that a tree cannot support the effects of sudden isolation several times without some degree of injury and loss of quality. Also we have to arrange for a progressive process of selection, because a large proportion, probably two-thirds, of the standards of two rotations old, will have to be eliminated as unfit for further reservation, and there will probably be only two or three trees per acre left of sufficient value to be worth reserving for four or five rotations. The prescription in our working-plan will therefore run somewhat as follows, taking these figures simply as an example: There will be reserved about forty standards of all ages per acre, and no tree, unless in exceptional circumstances, will be retained for more than four rotations (when they would probably be about 100 years old), and that at each felling about two-thirds of the number of standards of each age will be felled, and only the best retained. Then a rule embodying the well-known silvicultural conditions that control the selection of stems for reservation from out of the underwood, relating to species, origin, shape, etc., will be given, and lastly the distribution of the reserves must be remembered, and, if for example there are to be forty standards per acre, there should be four standards reserved on each square chain.

In the above example, there might be on every acre, twenty-seven standards of one rotation's age reserved from out of the underwood, nine standards of two rotations of age, and three standards of three rotations of age, which would ordinarily be felled at the close of their fourth rotation.

Prescriptions will then be drawn up for whatever subsidiary operations may be considered necessary. These will be cleanings and thinnings, which will be carried out by area on purely cultural lines. There may be one or two cleanings carried out while the underwood is still young, then one cleaning perhaps at mid-rotation, and a thinning about half-a-dozen years before the coppice is cut. The frequency and nature of these tending operations will depend entirely on cultural considerations, and on the light-requirements and relative rate of height-growth of the principal species. The rules should state the nature and object of each operation, but it is to be presumed that the forester in charge of the forest will have sufficient professional knowledge to carry out all ordinary operations in a fit and proper manner.

37. Methods included in even-aged high-forest.

Under the head of even-aged high-forest, there are a small number of variations of the method of treatment which will have to be considered separately. These are:

(1) The uniform method.
(2) The group method.
(3) Clear-felling with natural regeneration.
(4) Clear-felling with artificial regeneration.
(5) Strip-felling.

38. The Uniform method.

The uniform method of successive regeneration fellings, called in France the method of natural regeneration and thinnings, and in Germany the shelter-wood compartment system, is the typical method of even-aged high-forest management, and the group and strip methods are merely variations of it.

In this method the working-circle is divided into a few (generally about four to six) blocks of approximately equal area, each containing an equal range of age-classes. The number of blocks to be so formed is found by dividing the rotation by the number of years considered necessary under existing conditions to complete the regeneration of a block by successive regeneration fellings.

Thus, if it was estimated that about thirty-six years would be required to regenerate completely a block of mature crops under conditions where natural regeneration was rather difficult and slow, and the whole rotation was 144 years, there would have to be four blocks, and Block I would contain the crops forming the oldest quarter of the growing stock; or if the rotation were 100 years, and a period of twenty years was considered sufficient in which to regenerate a block, there would be five blocks. In this way the area is divided up into blocks corresponding to the same number of periods into which the rotation is sub-divided.

These blocks are therefore called periodic blocks, because each block is to be regenerated in the corresponding period, and the old mature crop replaced by a new crop of seedling growth during the course of the period. Block I, the oldest block, in the first period; Block II in the second period, and so on.

The first step then is to classify all the compartments and sub-compartments composing the working-circle, by age, and to arrange them by groups of ages into four or five blocks of equal or equiproductive area. This brings us to the question of whether these blocks are to be self-contained, that is, each of one holding, or whether they are to be composed of compartments scattered about all over the working-circle.

A compact block of a single holding is always a convenient and orderly feature of a plan, but it is not essential, and if such blocks can only be formed at the cost of many discrepancies in age-class, and consequently of the necessity of shifting a lot of crops about, out of their regular turn as indicated by their age, it is better to give up the idea of an entire block all of a single holding, and to be content with a block composed of crops of the requisite ages, scattered about over the forest.

(Note. In reviewing the different methods of treatment, we are going to pass over the matter of felling-series for the time being, for the sake of clearness. Except that each felling-series, which is necessarily self-contained as far as possible, must include a complete succession of all age-classes occupying equal areas, the formation of felling-series does not affect the method of treatment, and in the general working scheme it merely forms a detail regarding the location and distribution of the prescribed operations.)

Now since the principal fellings during any period are confined to the block corresponding, and as tending operations are meanwhile carried out in all the other periodic blocks alike, it might be sufficient to compose one block only at any given time, namely the block coming under regeneration, and to leave the separation of the other blocks to the future. For the duration of any given period it is only necessary to have the one block defined, and the three or four other blocks may be left to be arranged when their turn comes. A further step in the way of devolution now becomes visible, and, that is that, instead of having a fixed permanent periodic block, it would be sufficient, and might be advantageous, to have a floating block of approximately the same area, always formed of mature crops, most in need of regeneration, but revised and re-constituted say every ten years, so that at each decennial revision all areas in which the regeneration was completed would be thrown out, and fresh areas of the same extent fit for regeneration taken in. This *quartier bleu*, as it is called in France, differs from the ordinary periodic block in that it has not got to be regenerated during a time prescribed, but is an area composed of all the compartments in which regeneration fellings are to be either started or continued during the time. Provided that the rate of progress was suitably regulated by the prescriptions to determine the annual yield, the whole working-circle would in this way be worked through and progressively regenerated in a manner offering great elasticity to silvicultural conditions, though with a risk of some future disorder ensuing.

It is evident that, unless there is already a fairly regular succession of equal age-classes in the crop, the formation of the complete series which is required for each self-contained periodic block of equal area, will not readily be obtained, and in order to equalise the areas of the blocks it may be necessary, on account of its enforced topographical position, to include in one periodic block a compartment which, from the point of view of its age, ought to be placed in a different block. In such a case this compartment might have to be regenerated in a period other than that corresponding to the block in which it is of necessity placed. Absolute uniformity is not to be expected—at any rate until the second rotation. Then with regard to the internal subdivision of these periodic blocks, it is only in very exceptionally favourable circumstances that regular equal annual coupes can be laid out. The reason for this is that the regeneration does not proceed like clock-work, and that the successive regeneration fellings will necessarily depend for their progress on the gradual development of the young crop which is being created.

Good seed-years may only occur at infrequent intervals, and the regeneration must necessarily depend on cultural conditions, and cannot be forced. The yield therefore is nearly always regulated by volume, based on the cubic contents of the old standing crop which is to be removed within the period, and this annual volume may be extracted from any part of the block under regeneration, whether in the form of seed, secondary or final felling, according to silvicultural requirements. In the rare cases in which annual coupes can be laid out on the ground, the yield would be regulated by area, but the volume of timber becoming available year by year during the period would be easily ascertainable.

A general working scheme will then be drawn up for the whole rotation, and a tabular statement prepared showing what compartments have been allotted for regeneration to each period; and a special plan will be similarly prepared in tabular form showing the areas to be worked over during the coming period by regeneration fellings regulated by volume, and showing the ages of the crops occupying the compartments that form Block I. A table of the tending operations, cleanings and thinnings, according to cultural requirements, to be carried out over the whole working-circle during this same first period, indicating the periodicity of these operations, and the areas to be worked over each year up to the end of the period will also be prepared. These subsidiary fellings will be regulated by area only, but cultural rules may be issued, calling attention to any special features that may exist. The calculations on which is based the regulation of the annual yield will be discussed in the following chapter.

If the crop is a mixed one, rules will be issued applying both to the regeneration fellings and to the tending operations, laying down the cultural procedure to be followed in each case, so that the more valuable species may be protected against other competing kinds of trees, and favoured at each stage of its development. A judicious control of the light conditions will enable the forester to create a young crop of the composition desired, and to direct the development of the crop both in quantity and quality.

39. Clear-felling with natural regeneration.

Clear-felling, with natural regeneration is an exceptional method of treatment which is only possible under specially favourable circumstances. An instance occurs in the forests of the maritime pine in the sandy region of the Landes, in France.

This pine seeds freely every year, and reproduction takes place very easily on the loose sandy soil. The working of the forest is based entirely on area. Annual coupes are laid out, rectangular strips lying at right angles to the wind. Each year the coupe of the year is clear-felled, and the area regenerates itself naturally from seed on the ground. The working-plan lays down the procedure to be followed in tapping for resin. The rotation is seventy-five years. For the first fifty years, thinnings are made quinquennially, and the trees to be removed are tapped for one season before being felled. From fifty to seventy years of age the whole crop is tapped lightly, and then during the last five years before the felling, the trees are all tapped as intensively as possible. The forest is carefully fire-protected. The preparation of a working-plan for a pine forest worked for turpentine requires a detailed knowledge of the local conditions of soil and climate affecting the growth and regeneration of the pine, and also of the production of resin, and the best method of collecting it. This is an instance of a special industry in which commercial experience, as well as silvicultural knowledge, is necessary.

With local experience of these matters, the drafting of rules for a working-plan of this type of forest offers no particular difficulty, as the working scheme is a very simple one.

40. Clear-felling with artificial re-stocking.

This method, which is a very common one in Britain, is easy, but expensive, and is only suited to small areas, such as privately owned woodlands. There is often a danger of injury from insect pests. From the point of view of management, this method offers no difficulty. The yield would in most cases be regulated by area, on which basis the whole plan would be drawn up.

A plan of progressive clearing and re-planting by area would be drawn up for the next twenty years or so, while periodic tending operations and improvement fellings would have to be prescribed year by year for the other parts of the forest.

41. Strip-felling.

Strip-felling resembled clear-felling with natural regeneration, except that we have here a succession of regeneration fellings under a shelter-wood instead of a single clear-felling. The working is based on area, and the annual coupe is a long narrow strip usually placed at right angles to the direction of the wind, which is generally the controlling factor of the climate in the regions where this method is practised. The idea is to get side protection against wind, drought, frost and sun, combined with overhead light.

The forest is divided up into periodic blocks in the ordinary way, and a period of twenty or thirty years allotted for the regeneration of each block. The fellings, which consist of successive strips on which seed, secondary and find fellings, follow one another in due succession at intervals of a few years, always march against the wind, so that the young regeneration is sheltered by an old crop. If the wind conditions are severe, severance fellings must be made in advance to protect the leeward crops from being damaged by exposure to the wind.

This method is necessarily a rather rigid one, and in order to regulate the rate of progress of the regeneration to fit the period allotted, it will usually be convenient to institute a number of cutting-series, and at the same time to vary the width of the annual strip felled over. By a combination of these two expedients, the rate of progress of the regeneration can be controlled. It may, however, be often found necessary, in all probability, to supplement the natural regeneration by artificial re-stocking.

42. The Group method.

The group method is intermediate between the Uniform and the Selection methods, but is generally included among the methods applied to crops of mixed ages. It hardly forms a separate method of treatment, but is rather a silvicultural variation which may be applied either to the Selection method in crops of mixed ages (Group-Selection), or to the Uniform method in even-aged crops. In the latter case, the young crops resulting from this kind of regeneration felling will be less even-aged than those created under the Uniform method by compartments or by strips, and may contain groups of young growth varying by thirty years in age. This results from the fact that the regeneration area is generally larger than in the ordinary Uniform method, and the regeneration period considerably longer. The organisation of the working-circle, and the formation of periodic blocks, are the same. There will be of course no annual coupes laid out, but the possibility will be extracted from every part of the block under regeneration in which there are groups of young growth ready for extension. The annual yield is determined by volume, and the regeneration fellings will be progressively conducted all over the block during the period by purely cultural considerations, by the removal of the largest trees over advance growth, and by the subsequent expansion of these groups by the progressive extraction of the rest of the old stock. Preparatory and seed-fellings will often not be required, as the fellings may follow the regeneration instead of preceding it. All these points, however, are matters of silviculture rather than of management, and in the working-plan it will only be necessary to give effect to them in the rules prescribing the nature and mode of executing the fellings. Some provision may have to be made to facilitate the extraction of the old crop without damage to the surrounding young growth.

43. The Selection method.

The high-forest of mixed ages, worked by the Selection method, is, from the point of view of management, extremely simple.

Here we have the forest in its natural irregular condition; there is no artificial separation of age-classes, and there is no division of the area into periodic blocks. The whole forest is theoretically the same everywhere at any time, and any acre in it is exactly like any other acre, and contains trees of all ages from one year old up to the limit of the rotation. Since, however, in practice it is not possible to work over the whole area, which is often very extensive, every year, in order to pick out the trees which have just attained exploitable dimensions, a felling-cycle is adopted—generally between five and thirty years—and the forest is divided into a corresponding number of sections, one of which is worked over each year in succession. With a short felling-cycle the crop retains all the characteristic features of the irregular forest, while with a very long felling-cycle, it gradually approaches the even-aged type. The considerations which should determine the length of the felling-cycle are administrative and silvicultural. The annual sections or coupes should be of manageable size, and capable of effective supervision. Extraction and transport should be cheap and easy. Then taking into consideration the light-requirements of the principal species, the cycle should be such that no too great interval of years will lapse between two successive operations on any part, nor should it be so low that the crop will be fatigued and damaged by too frequent fellings. It will be noted that if a felling-cycle of twenty years, for example, be applied, we are going to harvest twenty years' accumulated production on one-twentieth of the area, instead of taking each year's production off the whole area.

The determination of the girth limit which is adopted as the size of maturity will result directly from the definition of the object of management, taken in conjunction with the size (easily ascertainable) of the firstly physical, and secondly commercial, maturity of the average tree.

The age corresponding to the size adopted as the exploitable size is obtained as the result of a large number of ring-countings of sample trees. The exploitable age, in round numbers, fixes the rotation, of which the felling-cycle will for convenience be generally taken as a sub-multiple.

Now although the constitution of the timber crop is hidden from our eyes, because the trees which form it are growing one above another, all mixed up in the utmost irregularity, there are two outstanding conditions which are necessary to enable the realisation of an equal annual yield in perpetuity: firstly, regeneration must be taking place every year without intermission on every acre of the area, and secondly there must be a complete and regularly graduated succession of all age-classes year by year, all occupying equal areas, all over the forest. This equal series of age-classes must exist although we cannot see it. In addition, for the annual yield to be a maximum, it is of course necessary that the forest should be fully stocked.

The only way in which the constitution of the crop can be ascertained is by making enumerations, and counting the number of stems in each group of size-classes. If the area of the working-circle, or felling-series, is small, we might make a complete enumeration, or if the area is too big, we should make a partial enumeration, either by sample plots, or, better, by linear surveys, all over the forest, and take countings over 5 or 10 per cent. of the whole area. These figures multiplied up will give us an estimate of the stock, and the proportion of the different groups of size-classes throughout the whole forest. An inspection of these gradated totals will at once tell us (more or less) if the succession of age-classes be anything like complete and regular, and we may have similar figures for other forests of the same kind, growing under similar conditions, with which to compare them.

It is possible, however, to gauge the corrections of the proportions in another way. If we represent graphically five groups of age-classes of equal area, as in the figure, the volumes of these five size-groups will be proportional to the five vertical columns *A*, *B*, *C*, *D*, and *E*, into which the triangle representing our whole growing stock, is divided; and these five areas evidently bear the proportion of 9 : 7 : 5 : 3 : 1. The volume of *A* then is $\frac{9}{25}$ of the whole; of *B*, $\frac{7}{25}$; and so on.

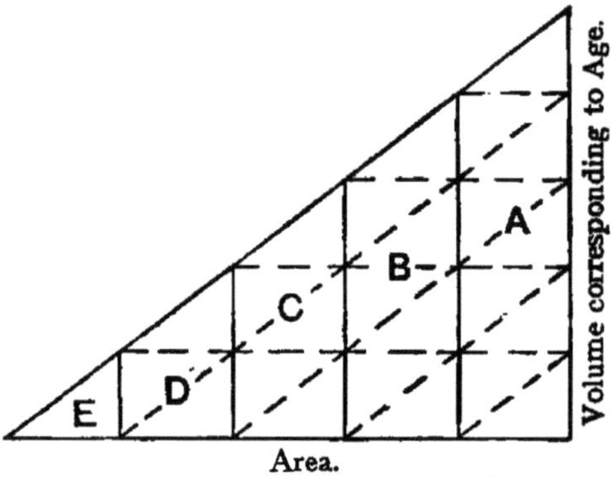

Now suppose that in the beech-woods of the Chiltern hills, it is known from a large number of past measurements, that the average stem of each of the following five size-groups contains the number of cubic feet given in the second column of the table here shown, and that the total volume per acre of a fully stocked crop is say 3000 cubic feet.

Per Acre.

Size-class Inches of quarter-girth	Volume of average tree of the class, cubic feet	Volume of whole size class, cubic feet	Numbe of trees in each size class	Percentage proportion of number of trees
0–3	0·25	120	480	54·4
3–6	1·50	360	240	27·25
6–9	7·30	600	82	9
9–12	19·40	840	44	5
12–15	29·60	1080	36	4·25
		3000	882	100

Under these local conditions of growth, this table gives us the percentage proportion of each group of size-classes, if the succession is complete and regular, and occupies equal areas.

It would not be very safe of course to take these figures for the very smallest size-class, which is the least easy and the least important to estimate, but we get some idea at any rate of the proper proportions that ought to exist, on every acre, of the larger and middle-sized classes. We might perfectly well work this out in greater detail by taking fifty or any other number of sizes, instead of making only five groups.

Another good method of ascertaining whether the relative proportions of the different age-classes are correct, is to plot a curve to represent these proportions after each enumeration. It is possible to plot a normal curve of this kind, and any deviation from the normal will at once be clearly indicated by comparison with it. This will show which age-classes are in excess, and which are deficient.

It is to be noted that under the Selection method the regeneration of the forest does not primarily depend on the fellings as it does in the even-aged forest. The principal fellings in the Selection method may often to some extent result in some local regeneration, and still more may they assist the development of young growth waiting to be uncovered, but they are not entirely responsible for the general regeneration of the forest, which should be taking place naturally and automatically over the whole forest all the time.

When the group method is applied to forests of mixed ages worked by the Selection method, mature trees are extracted by groups instead of by single stems, and these groups are subsequently expanded by later fellings, as the young growth in and around them develops. In this case the fellings bear the full character of regeneration fellings, although the natural regeneration is not confined to the areas actually included in these group fellings.

Under the Selection method, tending operations are generally of less importance than they are in even-aged crops. Unless, however, the felling-cycle is a very short one, of five or ten years, it will be necessary to carry out a cleaning or improvement felling, including the extraction of dead or dying trees, once at mid-period at least. In the year following the principal felling too, it may be found very beneficial to go over the same ground again with a cleaning, to cut back all young stems that have been broken or damaged in the previous year's exploitation, and to extract all bad and unmarketable material. A tabular statement will be prepared, showing for each year during the duration of the special plan what areas have to be worked over by these subsidiary operations year by year, and rules framed to state the nature of each kind of tending operation, its cultural objects, and the manner in which it is to be carried out. This tabular statement will be similar to the one prepared for the principal fellings, which also will be accompanied by cultural rules to supplement (and to take precedence of) the regulation of the yield—rules which are of the greatest importance, since they will touch on such fundamental matters as the maintenance of the leaf-canopy and of the fertility of the soil, the supply of seed, shelter against wind and exposure, favour shown to the more valuable species in the crop, etc.

44. Provisional methods.

The cases in which a provisional or temporary method of treatment has to be applied may be classified into two categories: first, there are the forests that for the future are to be worked under a new method of treatment, which renders it necessary to re-constitute the growing stock, and to arrange a different succession of age-classes to correspond with the new rotation; and secondly there are the forests of which the wood-capital is so deficient or so irregular that a preparatory period must be adopted during which this wood-capital may be improved and added to, until the growing stock has been sufficiently increased and completed to render it fit for working under a regular method of treatment. We have therefore to consider methods of (1) conversion, and (2) improvement.

The commonest and most important cases of conversion are from Coppice-with-standards to even-aged high-forest, and secondly from Selection to even-aged high-forest.

45. Conversion from Coppice-with-standards to Uniform.

In the case of conversion of Coppice-with-standards to the Uniform method, we have first of all to arrange for a preparatory period, during which the coppice will grow older, and so will gradually lose the power of reproducing itself, when cut, by stool-shoots. Then, when this period of waiting is over, we can begin to start the creation of the new series of age-classes by making regeneration fellings over a suitable area in that part of the forest which is most fit for it. The whole process of conversion cannot therefore be properly accompanied in a shorter time than the number of years in the preparatory waiting period plus the new rotation of the Uniform method. This total will probably be of the order of 150 to 200 years.

Now we have already agreed that we are not going to attempt to tackle so long a period as this in any working-plan. We are going to be content to provide, with a moderate degree of detail, for something like twenty, or at most thirty or thirty-five years, and we are not going to attempt to estimate results, or discuss figures, or put forward proposals in detail for such a lengthy future as 150 or 200 years.

Let us then suppose that the rotation under the coppice *régime* was 25 years, and that the rotation under the new Uniform method is to be 175 years divided into five periods of thirty-five years each, and let us suppose that the tree we principally have to deal with does not lose the power of reproducing itself freely by stool-shoots until it is at least sixty years old. Under these circumstances we should be led to take thirty-five years as the duration of the waiting period, so that at the end of that time our crop would be sixty years old and therefore fit to start regeneration fellings in.

Since, however, we have to convert the entire stock into a regular succession of ages, each occupying an equal area, we have got to conduct our regeneration fellings gradually year by year over the whole working-circle, and we cannot start them until thirty-five years have elapsed.

The programme of events will then be as follows: During the first period of thirty-five years we shall select one block, the one that is culturally in the best condition for the purpose, and carry out a few thinnings and minor cultural operations in it at intervals of eight or ten years while it grows older, and in the other four blocks we shall continue the coppice treatment. In the second period of thirty-five years, the regeneration of our first block will be started, a second block will be selected for submission to the waiting period, and coppice fellings will continue in the other three blocks. In the third period tending operations, cleanings and thinnings will be carried out in the now converted Block I, regeneration fellings will be taken through Block II, preparatory operations during the waiting period in Block III, and coppice fellings in Blocks IV and V.

There are thus four different kinds of operations going on now, and the whole process of conversion is going to take 210 years. This is the general scheme. Our working-plan, however, will only deal in detail with one period of thirty-five years. It is unnecessary here to discuss the nature of these four different kinds of operations, which are described in any book on silviculture. In the preparatory period they will consist principally in thinning out the coppice poles, so as to give the best of them more space to spread in. The regeneration fellings, and the subsequent tending operations in the coverted part of the area, will be similar to, if not identical with, such operations as commonly carried out in even-aged high-forest. The temporary coppice fellings continued in the later part of the area will be ordinary coppice fellings, but the rotation should be a long one, and in any case new coppice coupes will have to be laid out at the beginning of each period, as the area under coppice is gradually being reduced. Only in the case of the last coppice felling before a coppice area is brought under the waiting period, should the largest possible number of standards be reserved.

The above example shows an outline of the method to be followed in a plan of this sort, the general working scheme for the whole business, and the special plan for the period on which we are entering. The whole thing can be managed on a basis of area, even the regeneration (or conversion) fellings, unless natural regeneration is difficult, in which case the fellings can be made by volume and be carried out in any part of the block that is culturally fit for them, as in the ordinary Uniform method.

Tabular statements will be drawn up for each kind of operation, showing year by year throughout the period what areas have to be worked over, and rules will be framed to determine the nature of, and mode of execution of, each kind of felling. The whole operation is a cultural one, and considerable liberty should be left to the local operator with regard to the application of practical details.

Then, in addition to the four kinds of principal fellings going on in different parts of the area, there will also be subsidiary tending operations in each part; these will be cultural operations of a nature suitable to the condition of the crops and to the treatment that they are undergoing, and will be carried out with a periodicity suitable to their light-requirements, their density, composition, and condition.

46. Conversion from Selection to Uniform.

Conversion from irregular to regular high-forest is a process that every even-aged high-forest now worked under the Uniform method, or one of its variations, has had to pass through, since the natural forest is always composed of crops of all ages mixed up over the whole area and the even-aged condition is an artificial one.

Under certain well-known conditions the Selection method is a very excellent one, and offers scope for intensive working, but under other conditions, it is often desirable to introduce the regular Uniform method in order to obtain the great advantages that result from growing trees in close even-aged crops.

Theoretically the irregular high-forest is supposed to be of uniform irregularity all over, and one part is supposed to be exactly like another. In practice, however, this uniformity of irregularity (if the phrase be permissible) will not be found, and there will always be certain parts of the area containing a preponderance of old trees, other parts stocked principally with middle-aged trees, and other parts consisting largely—though of course not exclusively—of young growth.

Now in order to create a regular equal graduated succession

of even-aged crops over the whole area with which we are dealing, aged from one year old up to the age of exploitability, which is probably between 100 and 200 years old, it would seem at first sight necessary to spend an equal number of years to achieve this result. In practice this conversion may be completed in a considerably shorter period, because absolute uniformity is not attempted, and therefore a great deal of the younger growth already on the ground is left there to be incorporated in the new crop, although it will be of course really a good many years older.

During the process of conversion then, what we understand by an even-aged crop is not a crop composed entirely of trees of the same, or even approximately the same, age, but it is a crop sufficiently even-aged to be regenerated, when its time comes, in one set of regeneration fellings. Exact uniformity would entail also a great waste of production, and the sacrifice of a large quantity of immature stock, so we shall take a middle course and be satisfied for this first rotation if each part of the crop is mainly composed of trees within, say, about thirty years of the theoretical age.

The procedure then will be to examine carefully each compartment and sub-compartment, and to make enumerations over representative areas—either by linear surveys, or by sample plots—to ascertain the predominant proportion of size-class in each part of the crop, and we shall prepare a table to collate size with age. Then, after determining the rotation to be adopted under the new method of treatment, and having settled on a suitable period within which to complete the regeneration of any block, we shall form a general framework of the plan for conversion, allotting each unit of area—compartments and sub-compartments—to its appropriate period in this general scheme.

In periodic Block I, will be placed those parts of the crop in which regeneration is already abundant, and trees of the largest class numerous. In Block II, crops containing most class II trees, or class I and III trees, if class II trees are deficient; and so on.

In the last block will be placed the poorest and least satisfactory parts of the crop, which require to be nursed up and improved before their turn comes round for conversion. This general scheme for the allocation of each part of the crop to its most appropriate position in a periodic block is the most important part of the working-plan. The periodic blocks will have to be composed of areas scattered about all over the forest, and are not likely to be able to be compact self-contained areas. Periodic Block I will at once be brought under conversion, and regeneration fellings, regulated by area and cultural rules, will be carried out.

Seed fellings will probably be unnecessary, so we shall only make secondary and final fellings, in which all the old stock standing on the area in hand, down to, say, about three feet in girth, will gradually be removed. Everything below this limit will be left, if good, to form part of the new crop. If the cultural conditions of the regeneration permit it, it might be possible to prescribe the number of fellings and their periodicity, but as a rule such a prescription would be unwise.

This procedure would be based on the assumption that the conditions of regeneration were straightforward and easy; if this is not so, a less rigid method must be adopted, and instead of prescribing the number of fellings by area with a fixed periodicity, we must fix the possibility by volume, and instead of having defined annual coupes, we should make the regeneration fellings in any part of the block that was most ready for them, and be guided by the cultural requirements of each part.

A tabular statement showing the areas to be worked over year by year will be prepared for the duration of the first period, and a set of cultural rules, laying down the details of the manner in which these fellings are to be carried out, and providing what is, and what is not, to be felled, under special circumstances, will be carefully drawn up to accompany it. The operation being a purely cultural one, these rules will be of great importance, but they should be framed so as to allow some exercise of discretion to the officer who carries them out. Some subsidiary operations, such as cleanings and cutting-back, will be prescribed to follow the fellings in Block I.

Meanwhile in all the other blocks, selection fellings will be continued during the first period, at the end of which time

Block II will be brought under conversion and regenerated in the same way in the second period. These selection fellings will consist in removing mature stems which can be left standing no longer, but in addition to this they will go further, and will be improvement fellings in which worthless material of any size will be removed in order to assist in the development of the more valuable trees.

The position of every part of the forest in the general scheme of working being known, we shall know the girth limits of the trees to be specially favoured on each part of the ground in order to prepare the crop to take its place in the approaching conversion. These selection fellings therefore in the blocks not yet brought under conversion will aim at inducing to some extent a state of uniformity in the crops, and of regularising them to the type required to fit in with the conversion scheme.

47. Improvement method.

The Improvement method is a provisional treatment applied to forests which are in a very bad state, containing a large proportion of unsound and worthless timber, and therefore unfit, until to some extent restored, for working under any regular method. The object is therefore to improve the growing stock during a period of years, during which time the forest will be treated on purely cultural considerations, and no revenue be sought from it. During this provisional period, then, all trees, the extraction of which is culturally desirable, will be removed, but no others; and as a general rule no tree will be removed unless there is a better one to take its place. As a method of management, the arrangement will be exactly as under the Selection method. A suitable felling-cycle will be fixed, and the forest divided up into as many sections, over one of which an improvement felling will be carried out each year. In order that in the future there may be no intermission in the yield it is of course necessary to see that natural regeneration always continues to take place freely over the whole area year by year. There is no possibility fixed, and the fellings are carried out by area on purely silvicultural principles.

From the point of view of the working-plan, this method is of extreme simplicity: the most important features of the arrangement are the adoption of a felling-cycle of the (culturally) correct duration, and the cultural rules controlling the fellings.

These rules will state what timber is to be removed, and under what circumstances; they will also provide against too great reduction of the leaf-canopy, and of the density of the crops, and against over-exposure of young growth, and of the soil. Some subsidiary cultural operations may also be arranged in a second tabular statement showing the areas to be worked over year by year.

These minor operations and their periodicity will depend on the cultural requirements of the crop. In any case it will probably be wise to make one in the year following the principal improvement fellings, in which a cleaning will be made over the same area, and unsaleable material of all kinds extracted (all available marketable timber will have been taken out in the principal improvement felling and sold standing or felled), and all young growth of good species, but of bad shape, or damaged in the fellings, cut back. If the area is very large, several felling-series may be made in order to reduce the size of the annual coupe, as the felling-cycle should not usually be longer than twenty years at most.

CHAPTER VII. CALCULATION OF THE POSSIBILITY.

48. Theory and practice.

If everything were as it ought to be, the yield of the forest should be equal to the normal increment, that is, the maximum possible production per acre per annum under the rotation adopted, that the soil and climate permit. In highly organised forests where intensive working has been carried out for a long time, and where reliable yield-tables and increment-tables and exact statistical data of all kinds are available, the calculation of the possibility can be strictly worked out in accordance with the theory. In everyday practice, however, where such conditions rarely obtain, the regulation of the yield is generally calculated in a simpler and less theoretical fashion. This is especially the case when we have agreed to be content with short views, and to fix the yield only for twenty or thirty years, with a revision of the calculation every ten years. What actually happens in most cases is that we have a definite area to be worked over during a definite number of years, say twenty years for example, during which time we have to regenerate this area and to remove all the standing stock of old trees. We should then make an estimate of the actual volume of this mature crop, add on a trifle perhaps for future increment during the period, and then divide this total by the number of years, to get the annual yield for the period. This is the simplest method, and there is nothing theoretical in it.

The regulation of the yield may be by area, by volume, or by both.

49. Regulation by area.

First, by area. This is the method applied to coppice fellings, and to clear-fellings. The area under working is divided by the number of years in the rotation, and this gives the size of the annual coupe. If the site quality varies appreciably, the coupes may be made equiproductive rather than exactly equal in area. In the case of Coppice-with-standards, a further regulation has to be made with regard to the over-wood. To do this an estimate is made of the volume of timber which will be available during the coming rotation from the standards that will be extracted.

No rigid prescription as to the exact volume to be removed annually should issue, as there is always a good deal to be left to the appreciation of the local forester, with regard both to cultural and economic considerations, in dealing with the reservation and realisation of the standards.

50. Regulation by volume of growing stock.

Secondly, by volume. These methods are based either on the whole growing stock, or on the increment, or on both. The determination of the yield from the estimated volume of the whole wood-capital may be effected by dividing the total estimated cubic contents of the growing stock by half the number of years in the rotation. We have already considered this on page 9. This method may serve as a check to other methods but it is not very practicable, as it involves an enumeration of the whole growing stock, and is only true on the assumption that the actual increment bears to the actual growing stock the same relation as the normal increment bears to the normal growing stock.

51. Regulation by increment.

If the determination of the yield is based on increment, the average current annual increment may be obtained for each of four or five age classes, by using the borer on sample trees, or by felling and measuring sample trees; this average increment per acre is, if necessary, reduced by a factor for density, unless the whole area is fully stocked, and the increment thus modified is multiplied by the number of acres of each size or age-class, and the whole then totalled up, and divided by the number of acres in the felling-series. This method too is chiefly useful as a check on other methods.

Then lastly, if the yield is to be determined by volume, based on both increment and growing stock, it will be calculated by the formula

$$Y = \frac{i \, . \, x + (V - nV)}{x}$$

where i is the actual mean annual increment during an arbitrary time x, which is chosen as a convenient period for the distribution of the excess or deficiency of the actual growing stock as compared with the normal: V is the volume of the actual growing stock, and nV is found by multiplying the actual mean annual increment by half the number of years in the rotation.

In the statement of the formula given above, it is supposed that the actual growing stock is in excess of the normal growing stock, as may often be the case in virgin forests; but the difference between the volume of the actual growing stock and the normal growing stock corresponding to the actual mean annual increment may of course be either positive or negative.

52. Regulation by area and volume.

The best way, however, in everyday practice is to determine the yield on a basis of area combined with volume, and this is the method that will generally be employed in the Uniform method (except in the rare case when a succession of annual coupes can be employed and the working be arranged by area only, as mentioned on page 42), or in its variations, the Group, and the Strip methods.

Here we have a periodic block which is to be regenerated within the period of say twenty or thirty years. The yield is calculated solely with regard to this block and this period. Enumerations are made and an estimate is prepared of the actual growing stock, neglecting young growth if any exists.

Then the annual yield for this period will be $Y = \frac{V + \frac{1}{2}I}{p}$, where I is the future increment accruing during the period p, and V is the present volume of the actual standing crop which is to be extracted during the same period.

The reason for adding only one half of the increment expected to take place during the period is that the other half will remain on the ground after the passage of the fellings. If we have made our enumerations and estimates this year and make the first felling next year, we shall only realise one year's increment on the first coupe, and two years' increment on the second coupe, and so on, so that it will not be till we make the last felling of the period that we shall harvest twenty years' increment added on to the original volume. Thus for the whole period we shall harvest half the increment taking place over the whole periodic block during the whole period, the other half remaining in a succession of graduated crops on the ground after the passage of the fellings. The increment may be expressed either as a percentage of the growing stock, or as so many cubic feet per acre per annum. It is usual to make a rather low estimate of it, so as to keep on the safe side, and to have a reserve always in hand in case of accidents, such as wind storms, etc. Any excess of material is easily adjusted at the decennial revision.

53. French method.

In France, before making the calculation of the possibility based on an estimate of the volume of the mature crop to be removed during the coming period, it is customary to ascertain whether the older age-classes in the crop which will come under working in the near future, are approximately in correct gradation; so that, if desirable, an adjustment can be made in the regulation of the yield in case of any marked excess or deficiency in the older parts of the crop. This method is employed both with even-aged high-forest, and with Selection-worked forests.

Suppose for example that 6 feet in girth were adopted as the size of maturity; then an enumeration would be made, and the whole stock would be divided into three groups. The youngest, up to 2 feet in girth, the middle-aged third from 2 to 4 feet in girth, and the oldest third would include all stems of over 4 feet in girth. The estimated aggregate volumes of the oldest and of the middle-aged thirds would then be compared, and if they were found to bear respectively the ratio of five to three, it would be assumed that the age-classes were in sufficiently correct proportion.

This does not mean to say that the crop is necessarily by any means normal in volume, or fully stocked. This calculation is based on the method which we have already mentioned on page 46, and which may be graphically demonstrated by the figure, in which the volumes of the three thirds of the growing stock

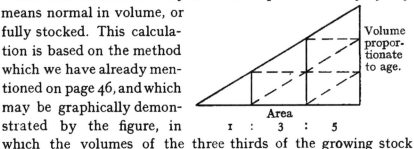

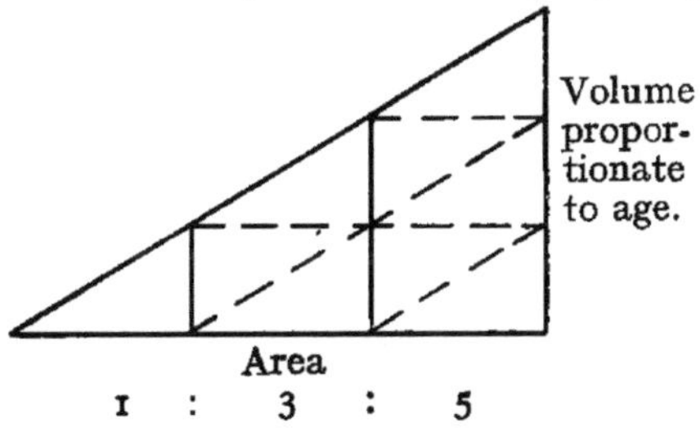

are relatively proportional to the three divisions of the triangle, and which therefore bear to one another the proportion of five to three, and three to one.

If now it is found that the proportion of five to three does not exist between the oldest and the middle-aged thirds of the crop, the difference is subtracted from the third in excess and added to the third showing deficiency, so as to obtain the correct proportion. When this adjustment has been made, the modified total volume of the oldest third, plus the addition of a modest increment for half the time, is divided by the number of years in one third of the rotation, and this gives the annual yield for that time. If timber extracted in thinnings or improvement fellings carried out in the middle-aged parts of the forest is of a size to bring it to be included in the possibility as prescribed, provision should be made for this in the calculation of the yield by adding to the total volume of timber in the oldest third of the crop a suitable proportion of the estimated future increment of the middle-aged third during the same period. In France the allowance for future increment is sometimes neglected, so as to keep well within the possibility, and to have a reserve always in hand wherewith to meet unforseen contingencies. This calculation of the annual yield is revised every ten years.

54. Calculation of yield under Selection method.

Under the Selection method we have already the following three limitations; firstly, area as determined by the size of the felling-series and the number of years in the felling-cycle adopted; secondly, a girth limit, which is the size adopted as the size of exploitability, on attaining which size each tree is fit for felling; and thirdly, cultural rules, which, although they are of paramount importance, do not directly affect the present calculation. Now it is evident that the first two limitations already define exactly the annual yield, so that it is unnecessary in addition to prescribe a fixed number of trees. It is, however, usually convenient to know what the average annual out-turn is going to be, but this number of trees cannot logically be enforced by a rigid prescription, though it may be prescribed as a maximum, if there is any object in so doing, or given merely as a general guide to the conduct of the annual working.

This possibility may be calculated as follows: An enumeration is made of the whole stock, either by actual counting or by estimate, and the number of stems in each of four or five size-groups is ascertained. Suppose for example that 6 feet in girth is taken as the size of maturity, then all trees of 6 feet or over form Class I. Class II includes all trees with a girth between $4\frac{1}{2}$ and 6 feet, Class III includes all stems between 3 feet and $4\frac{1}{2}$ feet in girth, and so on. It has also to be ascertained by ring countings how many years the average tree takes to pass from one class to the next. Knowing then the number of trees in Class II, and the number of years it will take the whole of this number to pass up into the exploitable Class I, we can easily calculate the annual rate of production of trees of the exploitable size. The number of trees in Class II has only to be divided by the number of years that it takes a tree to pass through that class.

This number forms the basis of our calculation of the yield, which, it is to be noted, is not based on the existing number of Class I trees (as might, at first sight, seem natural), because the number of trees in Class I is purely accidental, depending on past fellings, and tells us nothing as to the future rate of production annually of trees of the required size.

There is, however, a further point to be considered. We do not propose to fell over the whole area every year, but we have chosen a felling-cycle, of, for example, twenty years, so that we are going to confine our operations each year to one-twentieth of the area, and we can only realise the production of the whole forest off one-twentieth of its area on the condition that we have twenty years' accumulation of production standing, waiting for the fellings to come round. It is evident therefore that we must have twenty years' accumulation of Class I trees on one coupe, nineteen years' accumulation on the next coupe, and so on down to one year's production of Class I trees on the area worked over last year. We shall therefore have to keep a considerable stock of Class I trees, in regular gradated succession, always standing. The point that we now have to consider is whether the existing stock of Class I trees will be sufficient or not for this purpose during the first rotation. The total number of Class I trees that we require as a working exploitable stock is the number of trees becoming annually exploitable,—which we have already found as the basis of our calculation of the yield,—multiplied by half the number of years in the felling-cycle. This number then has to be compared with the figure showing the number of Class I trees in our table of enumeration, and any excess or deficit spread out over a suitable number of years, and added to, or deducted from, the original number of trees passing annually from Class II to Class I.

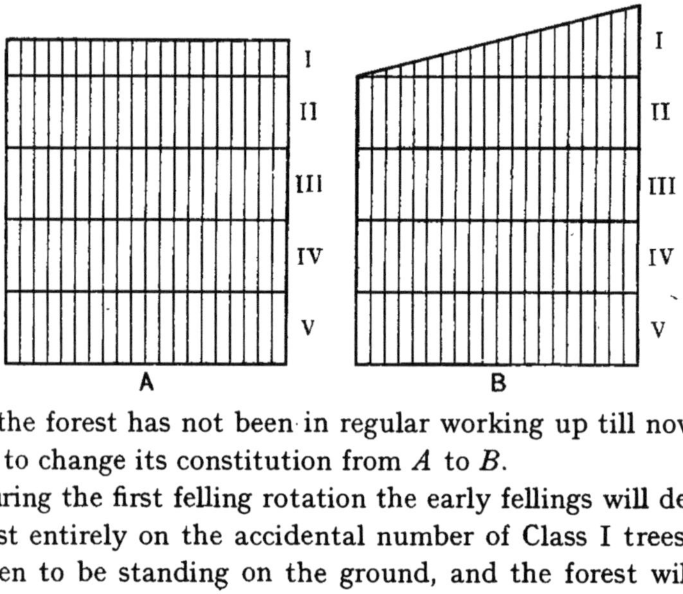

A B

If the forest has not been in regular working up till now, we have to change its constitution from *A* to *B*.

During the first felling rotation the early fellings will depend almost entirely on the accidental number of Class I trees that happen to be standing on the ground, and the forest will not come into full and regular production of an equal maximum annual yield until the second felling-cycle, when the full succession of the necessary exploitable stock will be completely constituted.

It will be noted that the average age of the trees forming the yield will be greater than the exploitable age by half the number of years in the felling-cycle.

CHAPTER VIII. THE WORKING-PLAN REPORT.

55. Form of report.

THERE is no stereotyped form of report for general use, and the size of the report and the amount of detail it contains must obviously depend upon the size and importance of the forest, and on the complexity of its component parts. With this provision, the form of the report will usually be more or less as here given.

PART I. SUMMARY OF FACTS ON WHICH THE PROPOSALS ARE BASED.

CHAPTER I. DESCRIPTION OF THE TRACT.

Name. Ownership. Situation.
Configuration of the ground. Elevation.
Soil and subsoil.
Climate.

CHAPTER II. COMPOSITION AND CONDITION OF FOREST.

Distribution and area. Existing subdivisions.
State of boundaries. Adjoining properties.
General description of crops, with silvicultural notes regarding species and their regeneration.
Legal position of forests. Rights and concessions.
Sources of injury. Wind, frost, fire, game, insect and fungoid pests, weeds.

CHAPTER III. MANAGEMENT.

Past and present methods of treatment. Results.
Special works of improvement.
Past revenue and expenditure.

CHAPTER IV. UTILISATION OF PRODUCE.

Marketable products. Classification and prices. Lines of export; method and cost of extraction. Local industries. Centres of consumption and markets.

CHAPTER V. MISCELLANEOUS FACTS.

Labour supply.
Forest staff.

PART II. FUTURE MANAGEMENT.

CHAPTER I. ALLOTMENT OF AREAS AND ANALYSIS OF THE CROPS.

Division of area into working-circles and felling-series. Reasons for their formation.

Formation of compartments and sub-compartments.

Enumerations carried out.

Their result. Distribution of age-classes.

CHAPTER II. BASIS OF MANAGEMENT.

Object of management.

Choice of species and silvicultural treatment.

Choice of rotation.

CHAPTER III. THE FELLINGS.

General working scheme.

Special plan for the period.

Determination of the annual yield.

Tabular felling statement of annual areas.

Cultural rules for execution of fellings.

CHAPTER IV. TENDING OPERATIONS.

Tabular statement of annual areas to be worked over by subsidiary improvement fellings, cleanings, thinnings, sowings and plantings.

Fire-protection.

Miscellaneous prescriptions.

CHAPTER V. SUPPLEMENTARY PROVISIONS.

Roads, buildings, and other works: plan of execution.

Collection of data. Upkeep of records of sample plots and measurements.

Organisation of forest staff.

Forecast of financial results.

Revisions.

APPENDICES.

Description of compartments and sub-compartments.

Maps.

Enumeration surveys, with map.

Record of measurements for compiling yield-tables, and increment-tables.

Results of ring-countings and borings.

Miscellaneous.

Part I of the plan deals with the past and present, and Part II with the future.

Part I will therefore contain no prescription or provision for the future, which will all be given in their appropriate place in Part II. In Part II, the basis of future management is the object of management as defined, and from this are deduced successively the species (if any choice is possible), the method of treatment, and the size of maturity under the object of management, from which again is deduced the rotation. These sections should be written coherently and logically, in concise and exact terms.

Chapters II, III and IV have to be written separately for each working-circle.

56. Control Form and Forest Journal.

A working-plan is not of much use unless its prescriptions are carried out. The control book is a means of ensuring continued adhesion to the plan, and at the same time it forms a record of the progress of the forest under the working-plan. It is mostly kept in tabular form, with one book for each working-circle, and one page (or more if necessary), for each year.

On the left-hand page is a table prepared showing in detail the provisions of the plan; principal fellings, subsidiary fellings, cultural operations, roads, buildings and works of all kinds, in each locality, with the acreage of each, with the quantity of material to be extracted, or expenditure to be incurred, are set forth in tabular form for the year under review. On the right-hand page opposite, a similar table is presented, in which are filled in corresponding entries, showing what has been actually done under each heading, and what operations have been carried out, and their result in material and in money. A brief statement is made to explain each deviation from the provisions of the plan, and the reasons for the non-fulfilment in whole or in part, of any operation prescribed. Any changes in area are recorded. This control book is prepared each year at the close of the working season by the forester in charge, and submitted to the owner of the forest for his approval and orders.

An abstract of the results of the year's working in timber and other produce, and a similar financial return for the year's revenue and expenditure, with the results compared with previous years' figures, should be drawn up at the same time.

A Forest Journal should also be kept up year by year in which an informal record will be kept, in narrative form, of all matters of interest connected with the forest and its working, which are not already recorded in the control form. Silvicultural notes of all kinds, especially on regeneration, will be put on record, also anything remarkable in the way of climate, such as wind, storms, frost, snow, or drought: then fires; fluctuations of prices, special demands for any kind of produce, contractors, and labour supply, etc. As a record of cultural observations, and notes on the regeneration and growth of the crops under the changing conditions of each season's climate, the journal, if well kept, forms a most valuable record of information for future use.

57. Outline of plan of management.

In the management of a British woodland estate, the general principle is the same as in a large State forest, and that is, to get the area fully stocked with the most suitable and profitable species, and therefore to realise annually a constant maximum yield equal to the mean annual increment, which will give the greatest annual revenue. This, continued with the least possible annual expenses, will result in the highest rent from the soil. Two conditions are necessary to start with—continuity of management for at least one or two human generations, and a definite object of management. Both these conditions often do not exist, and even where they do, there will be often an insufficiently stocked wood-capital and a very incomplete series of age-classes. In such a case the working-plan, which will be an organised attempt to convert the actual into the ideal, can only be drawn up on very elastic principles and will aim at getting the area completely stocked in the least possible time, with annual receipts meanwhile to cover annual expenses. If a plan can include several estates in the same district, it will be very advantageous to arrange an organised supply of timber for the local timber market, and for the producers to combine to maintain a steady and attractive market, instead of each selling separately at any price that the local trader likes to give him.

The preparation of the plan will be carried out in the way that has been already indicated for other forests. A general survey of the area will first be made, and some improvements may at once suggest themselves with regard to the choice of species and of method of treatment in different parts of the area. The first object should be to maintain and improve the productive capacity of the soil. The area will then be divided up into compartments (and sub-compartments if necessary), which should usually have a road or ride along one side, and should be of five to twenty acres in extent. Working-circles will then be formed, and the crops in each will be classified by age and condition into say five age-groups of about twenty years each.

Most of the crops of about eighty years old or over will be put into Block I to be dealt with during the first period of twenty years or thereabouts. The general working scheme may be rather less rigidly laid down here than it is for a large State forest worked on a long rotation.

Block I, then, will be composed of all the old mature or over-mature crops, which are often numerous in neglected woods, and other areas which are in such an unsatisfactory state that they too should be soon cleared and replanted. An estimate will now be made of the volume of material to be extracted by successive annual or periodical fellings during the first period. A tabular felling statement showing the areas to be taken in hand year by year will be drawn up, and the allotment of the different areas will be made in consideration of the condition of each crop, and the urgency of clearing it. A second table will be drawn up for cultural operations, and works of improvement, cleanings and thinnings, in the other parts of the forest.

Simplicity and economy should be the chief features of the plan, which should result in a steady progression, annual or periodical, towards clearing and replanting in systematic succession, with equalised working. No unregulated fellings for estate or any other purposes should be permitted. No high theory, nor abstruse calculations are required, but only a common-sense programme of operations; if, as will most often be the case, the re-stocking of the cleared areas is to be artificially carried out by sowing or planting, an annual plan of these operations will be required, and provision should be made for a nursery of adequate size in the most suitable locality. Cultural considerations to be followed should be clearly indicated, but the prescriptions should not be too rigid in matters of detail.

INDEX

CAMBRIDGE: PRINTED BY J. B. PEACE, M.A., AT THE UNIVERSITY PRESS.

* 9 7 8 1 3 3 2 3 4 1 1 5 3 *
SD - #0030 - 210921 - C0 - 229/152/5 - PB - 9781332341153